GW01339156

0006909
STALHAM HIGH SCHOOL

CHILDREN'S CLASSICS
EVERYMAN'S LIBRARY

The Everyman Anthology of Poetry for Children

Compiled by Gillian Avery
with illustrations by Thomas Bewick

EVERYMAN'S LIBRARY
CHILDREN'S CLASSICS

This selection by Gillian Avery first published in
Everyman's Library 1994
© David Campbell Publishers Ltd., 1994

A list of acknowledgments to copyright owners appears
at the back of this volume

Book design by Barbara de Wilde, Carol Devine Carson and Peter B. Willberg
Design and typography © David Campbell Publishers Ltd., 1994

Five of Ernest H. Shepard's illustrations from *Dream Days* by Kenneth
Grahame are reprinted on the endpapers by permission of The Bodley Head,
London. The sixth illustration is by S.C. Hulme Beaman.

ISBN 1-85715-931-4

A CIP catalogue record for this book is available from the British Library

Published by David Campbell Publishers Ltd.,
Gloucester Mansions, 140A Shaftesbury Avenue
London WC2H 8HD

Distributed by Random House (UK) Ltd.,
20 Vauxhall Bridge Road, London SW1V 2SA

Printed and bound in Germany by
Graphischer Grossbetrieb Pössneck GmbH

Contents

PREFACE xix

RHYMES AND NONSENSE

ANONYMOUS Gray Goose 3
ANONYMOUS The Boatman 3
ANONYMOUS I Had a Little Castle 3
ANONYMOUS The Bellman's Song 4
ANONYMOUS The Owl 4
BEN JONSON A Catch 5
ANONYMOUS The Man in the Wilderness 5
ANONYMOUS I'll Bark against the Dog-Star 6
ANONYMOUS The Merry Bells of London 6
ANONYMOUS Upon Paul's Steeple 8
ANONYMOUS Trip upon Trenchers 8
ANONYMOUS A Man of Words 9
ANONYMOUS White Bird Featherless 9
ANONYMOUS The Key of the Kingdom 10
ANONYMOUS The Frog and Mouse 11
ANONYMOUS Three Young Rats 12
ANONYMOUS The Fox's Raid 13
ANONYMOUS The Drunkard and the Pig 14
ANONYMOUS Black Sheep 15
ANONYMOUS Sisters 15
ANONYMOUS There was a Monkey 16
WILLIAM MAKEPEACE THACKERAY A Tragic Story 17
LEWIS CARROLL The Three Badgers 18
EDWARD LEAR The Table and the Chair 20
LAURA RICHARDS The Owl and the Eel and the Warming-Pan 21
EDWARD LEAR Calico Pie 22
JAMES WHITCOMB RILEY Craqueodoom 23
ANONYMOUS The Foolish Boy 24

vii

ANONYMOUS I Sometimes Think 25
ANONYMOUS The Common Cormorant 26
VACHEL LINDSAY Two Old Crows 27
ANONYMOUS Clementine..................................28
ANONYMOUS The Eddystone Light........................29

THE YEAR AND ITS SEASONS

OGDEN NASH It's Never Fair Weather 33
ANONYMOUS A New Year Carol............................34
SHU HSI *trans.* Arthur Waley Hot Cake 35
WILLIAM SHAKESPEARE Winter..........................35
JOHN KEATS *From* The Eve of St Agnes......................36
ROBERT BRIDGES London Snow..........................37
THOMAS HARDY Birds at Winter Nightfall..................39
              Winter in Durnover Field 39
ROBERT GRAVES Star-Talk 40
WALTER DE LA MARE The Scarecrow 41
ROBERT HERRICK Ceremonies for Candlemass Eve 42
CHARLES CAUSLEY At Candlemas 43
IVOR GURNEY When March Blows.........................44
WILLIAM SHAKESPEARE Spring 44
THOMAS HARDY Weathers................................45
JOHN CLARE Spring 46
CHRISTOPHER SMART Mirth 47
WILLIAM WORDSWORTH A Summer's Day 48
EMILY DICKINSON Answer July 49
ROBERT FROST The Oven Bird............................50
CH'ENG HSAIO *trans.* Arthur Waley
  Satire on Paying Calls in August 51
SEAMUS HEANEY Blackberry-Picking......................52
EMILY DICKINSON The Wind Began to Rock the Grass......53
JOHN KEATS To Autumn 54

viii

TED HUGHES The Harvest Moon 55
SYLVIA PLATH Mushrooms 56
SIR JOHN BETJEMAN Harvest Hymn..................... 57
DAVE GOULDER The Long and Lonely Winter 58
JOHN CLARE Autumn 59
ALFRED, LORD TENNYSON To-night the Winds Begin to
  Rise... 60
FRANCES CORNFORD Acrostic for Guy Fawkes Night....... 61
ROBERT SOUTHWELL New Prince, New Pomp 62
ROBERT HERRICK Ceremonies for Christmas 63
GEORGE HERBERT Christmas 64

JOURNEYS AND PLACES

ANONYMOUS The Shepherd Boy's Carol.................. 69
T. S. ELIOT Journey of the Magi........................ 71
ROBERT HAYDEN *From* Runagate, Runagate 73
JAMES D. RUBADIRI Stanley Meets Mutesa................ 74
ROBERT FROST The Road Not Taken 77
EDWARD THOMAS The Green Roads 78
ALFRED, LORD TENNYSON *From* The Lady of Shalott 79
RUDYARD KIPLING The Way Through the Woods 80
G. K. CHESTERTON The Rolling English Road 81
JAMES ELROY FLECKER The Old Ships 82
EMILY DICKINSON I Like to See it Lap the Miles........... 83
W. H. AUDEN Night Mail 84
EDWARD THOMAS Adlestrop 86
FRANCES CORNFORD Travelling Home 87
STEPHEN VINCENT BENET American Names.............. 88
ROBERT LOUIS STEVENSON In the Highlands 90
ELIZABETH BISHOP The Map 91
EDWARD THOMAS If I Should Ever by Chance 92
            What Shall I Give?...................... 93

GERARD MANLEY HOPKINS Binsey Poplars................ 94
WILLIAM WORDSWORTH Composed Upon Westminster
  Bridge.. 95
T. S. ELIOT Landscapes 95

SPELLS, MAGIC AND MYSTERY

JAMES REEVES Spells 101
ANONYMOUS I Have Four Sisters Beyond the Sea.......... 102
WILLIAM SHAKESPEARE Ariel's Songs 103
                     Fairy Songs................... 104–5
                     Puck's Epilogue 106
JOHN DONNE Song... 107
SIR WALTER SCOTT Lucy Ashton's Song 108
SAMUEL TAYLOR COLERIDGE Kubla Khan 108
WALTER DE LA MARE Song of the Mad Prince 110
WILLIAM SHAKESPEARE Witches' Song................... 111
BEN JONSON The Witches' Charms 112
ROBERT LOUIS STEVENSON Windy Nights............... 114
CHRISTINA ROSSETTI *From* Goblin Market............... 114
W. B. YEATS The Stolen Child 117
ANONYMOUS Two Corpus Christi Carols 119
ANONYMOUS from the Xhosa *trans.* A. C. Jordan Thou Great God... 121

STRANGE TALES

ANONYMOUS There was a Lady all Skin and Bone 125
ANONYMOUS The Wife of Usher's Well.................... 126
ANONYMOUS Strange Company........................... 128
JAMES HOGG Kilmeny Returns from the Land of the Spirits . 130
JOHN MASEFIELD The Rider at the Gate.................. 131
CHARLES CAUSLEY Miller's End 134
ELIZABETH JENNINGS The Secret Brother 135

x

BRIAN PATTEN You'd Better Believe Him 136
ROBERT HAYDEN A Road in Kentucky.................... 137
JAMES WHITCOMB RILEY Little Orphant Annie 139

MUSIC AND DANCING

WILLIAM SHAKESPEARE How Sweet the Moonlight Sleeps . 143
JOHN MILTON *From* Comus................................ 143
JOHN DRYDEN *From* A Song for St Cecilia's Day 145
PERCY BYSSHE SHELLEY Hymn of Pan.................. 146
ALFRED, LORD TENNYSON The Splendour Falls on Castle
   Walls... 148
LEWIS CARROLL The Mock Turtle's Song 149
W. B. YEATS The Fiddler of Dooney 149
KOJO GYINAYE KYEI The Talking Drums 150
LANGSTON HUGHES Danse Africaine.................... 152
HILAIRE BELLOC Tarantella 153
EDITH SITWELL Polka 154
SYDNEY CARTER Lord of the Dance...................... 156

BATTLES, SOLDIERS AND PATRIOTS

JAMES ELROY FLECKER War Song of the Saracens 161
GEORGE GORDON, LORD BYRON The Destruction of
   Sennacherib 162
SIR WALTER SCOTT Pibroch of Donuil Dhu 163
THOMAS BABINGTON, LORD MACAULAY A Jacobite's
   Epitaph 165
ROBERT BROWNING The Patriot 166
RUDYARD KIPLING A St Helena Lullaby 167
GEORGE GORDON, LORD BYRON The Eve of Waterloo 169
                            Napoleon's Farewell..... 171
WALT WHITMAN O Captain! My Captain! 172

RUDYARD KIPLING Tommy 173
WILFRED OWEN Anthem for Doomed Youth 175
RUDYARD KIPLING Epitaphs on the War: The Coward...... 175
WILFRED OWEN Disabled 176

BIRDS AND BEASTS

ANONYMOUS The Cuckoo is a Merry Bird.................. 181
ANONYMOUS Cuckoo, Cuckoo 182
ANONYMOUS Sweet Suffolk Owl 183
ALFRED, LORD TENNYSON The Owl..................... 183
JOHN CLARE Autumn Birds............................... 184
CELIA THAXTER The Sandpiper......................... 185
DAVID McCORD Crows................................... 186
ALFRED, LORD TENNYSON The Eagle 187
EMILY DICKINSON The Spider.......................... 187
JOHN CLARE The Vixen................................... 188
            Hares at Play 189
ANTHONY THWAITE Hedgehog 189
OLIVER GOLDSMITH An Elegy on the Death of a Mad Dog . 190
ALEXANDER POPE Epigram on the Collar of a Dog 192
NORMAN MacCAIG Praise of a Collie 192
THOMAS GRAY Ode on the Death of a Favourite Cat 193
ANONYMOUS from the Gaelic *trans.* Robin Flower Pangur Bán...... 195
W. B. YEATS The Cat and the Moon 196
T. S. ELIOT The Naming of Cats......................... 197
WILLIAM COWPER Epitaph on a Hare 198
ANONYMOUS Epitaph on a Dormouse 200
MARJORY FLEMING Sonnet to a Monkey 201
HILAIRE BELLOC The Frog 201
HILAIRE BELLOC The Python............................ 202
RUDYARD KIPLING Road-Song of the *Bandar-Log*.......... 203
WILLIAM BLAKE The Tyger 204

ANONYMOUS Two Yoruba Poems *trans.* Ulli Beier 205
ANONYMOUS Dick Turpin's Ride on Black Bess 206
PHILIP LARKIN At Grass................................207
                  First Sight 209
G. K. CHESTERTON The Donkey........................209
RICHARD WILBUR Francis Jammes: A Prayer to go to Paradise
   with the Donkeys 210
WALT WHITMAN The Ox-Tamer........................211
THOMAS HARDY The Oxen 213
CHARLES CAUSLEY Carol of Birds, Beasts and Men.........213

CHILDHOOD AND YOUTH

OGDEN NASH It is indeed Spinach 219
                  Children's Party...........................220
SIR JOHN BETJEMAN Indoor Games near Newbury.........221
SIR JOHN BETJEMAN Hunter Trials.....................223
ANONYMOUS from the Yoruba *trans.* Ulli Beier Praise of a Child....224
ROBERT HERRICK To his Saviour, a Child 225
WILLIAM BLAKE The Echoing Green....................225
                  Laughing Song 227
THOM GUNN Baby Song 227
ANONYMOUS from the Yoruba *trans.* Ulli Beier Yoruba Lullabies....228
THOMAS DEKKER Lullaby..............................229
MIKHAIL YURIEVICH LERMONTOV *trans.* Cornford and
   Salaman Cossack Lullaby...............................230
RICHARD CORBET To his Son, Vincent Corbet.............232
HUGH PETERS Wishes for his Daughter 233
LOUIS MacNEICE Autobiography........................234
GEORMBEEYI ADALI-MORTTI Palm Leaves of Childhood ..235
PETER ABRAHAMS Me, Colored 236
FRANCES CORNFORD Childhood.......................238
RICHARD WILBUR Boy at the Window...................239

ANTHONY THWAITE White Snow 240
DAVID McCORD The Game............................. 241
ANONYMOUS The Birched Schoolboy 242
WILLIAM BLAKE The Schoolboy 243
ROBERT FROST Birches................................ 245
SIR NOEL COWARD The Boy Actor...................... 247
ANONYMOUS A Daughter's Song 249
OGDEN NASH Daddy's Home, See You To-morrow 250
JOHN CROWE RANSOM Blue Girls 251
CHARLES CAUSLEY Who?.............................. 251
ROBERT HERRICK Epitaph upon a Child that Died......... 252
DONALD JUSTICE On the Death of Friends in Childhood ... 253

SOME PEOPLE

WILLIAM SHAKESPEARE The Seven Ages of Man 257
ANONYMOUS The Bonnie Earl of Moray 258
RUDYARD KIPLING The Looking-Glass 259
BEN JONSON Epitaph on Salathiel Pavy..................... 260
COLLEY CIBBER The Blind Boy........................... 261
JOHN O'KEEFFE The Little Plough-Boy 262
OLIVER GOLDSMITH The Village Schoolmaster 263
WILLIAM WORDSWORTH The Solitary Reaper............. 264
LANGSTON HUGHES Negro.............................. 265
PADRAIC COLUM An Old Woman of the Roads 266
LANGSTON HUGHES Aunt Sue's Stories.................... 267
GWENDOLYN BROOKS The Ballad of Rudolph Reed 268
EDWARD LEAR Self-Portrait of Edward Lear................ 270
W. H. AUDEN Edward Lear 272
WILLIAM PLOMER A Victorian Album..................... 273
HILAIRE BELLOC Peter Goole, who Ruined his Father and
    Mother by his Extravagance........................... 274
E. V. RIEU Sir Smasham Uppe........................... 276

SAMUEL TAYLOR COLERIDGE Epigram on a Singer........277
FRANCES CORNFORD Post-Bore Triolet...................278
SIR WALTER A. RALEIGH Wishes of an Elderly Man........278
JOHN WILMOT, EARL OF ROCHESTER Impromptu on
   Charles II 278
WALTER SAVAGE LANDOR The Georges..................279
THOMAS BROWN Lines to the Head of his College 279
SEAMUS HEANEY Follower 279

LOVE AND LOVERS' TALES

ANONYMOUS Bridal Morning 283
ANONYMOUS Western Wind 283
ANONYMOUS from the Latin *trans.* Helen Waddell Down from the
   Branches...284
ANONYMOUS I Know Where I'm Going 285
ANONYMOUS The Water is Wide.........................286
ANONYMOUS The Cambric Shirt.........................287
HENRY CAREY Sally in Our Alley 288
ROBERT LOUIS STEVENSON Romance 290
LOUISE BOGAN The Crossed Apple 291
WILLIAM SHAKESPEARE To Me, Fair Friend, You Never
   Can Be Old..293
SIR PHILIP SIDNEY My True Love Hath My Heart.........293
ANONYMOUS Hynd Horn................................294
ANONYMOUS The Gay Goshawk..........................297
EZRA POUND The River-Merchant's Wife: A Letter 300
CHARLES DIBDIN The Lady's Diary 301
SIR WALTER SCOTT Lochinvar..........................303
EDITH SITWELL The Little Ghost who Died for Love......305
ANONYMOUS Frankie and Johnny 307
LEWIS CARROLL The King-Fisher's Song..................311
LAURA RICHARDS Antonio 312

SIR JOHN SUCKLING Why so Pale and Wan? 313

LAST THINGS

ANONYMOUS Matthew, Mark, Luke, and John 317
SIR THOMAS BROWNE Evening Hymn 317
WILLIAM BLAKE Night 319
WILLIAM SHAKESPEARE Wolsey's Farewell 321
JOHN MILTON On his Blindness 322
JOHN KEATS When I Have Fears That I May Cease To Be ... 322
PERCY BYSSHE SHELLEY *From* Adonais 323
SIR WALTER SCOTT Proud Maisie 325
PERCY BYSSHE SHELLEY Ozymandias 325
WILLIAM WORDSWORTH On the Extinction of the
  Venetian Republic, 1802 326
A. E. HOUSMAN On Wenlock Edge 327
WILLIAM SHAKESPEARE Dirge for Fidele 328
CHRISTINA ROSSETTI Remember 329
ROBERT LOUIS STEVENSON Requiem 329
ALFRED, LORD TENNYSON I Climb the Hill 330
WILLIAM (JOHNSON) CORY Heraclitus 331
WILLIAM WORDSWORTH One Christmas-Time 331
COVENTRY PATMORE A London Fête 333
EMILY DICKINSON Because I Could Not Stop For Death ... 334
SIR JOHN BEAUMONT To my dear Son, Gervase Beaumont . . 335
JOHN OLDHAM A Quiet Soul 336
JOHN CROWE RANSOM Janet Waking 337
EDWIN MUIR The Child Dying 338
THOMAS HARDY Afterwards 339
  The Garden Seat 340
ROBERT FROST In a Disused Graveyard 341
WILLIAM SHAKESPEARE Prospero's Farewell to his Magic ... 342
  Macbeth on Lady Macbeth's Death ... 342

HENRY VAUGHAN Peace 343
JAMES ELROY FLECKER To a Poet a Thousand Years Hence 343

Acknowledgments... 345
Notes 347
Index of Authors and Titles 357
Index of First Lines 371

PREFACE

My aim has been to assemble a collection of poems that the owner will not outgrow. I have avoided those deliberately aimed at youth which – with the exception of nonsense – tend to be worthy and dull, if not arch and fey. One of the reasons why so much of it fails to appeal is that those writers who are not teaching moral truths are wrestling to bring their matter down to child level. Whereas, as Dr Johnson remarked, 'babies do not want to hear about babies; they like to be told about giants and castles'. This is why the Mother Goose rhymes have always been so successful. Sometimes magical and mysterious, sometimes comic, bawdy or frightening, they have brought a unique richness to English literature, and have for centuries been most English-speakers' first experience of poetry. But only a handful – as the Opies have shown – were ever intended for children (or indeed feature children) and those that were seem pallid and wishy-washy beside, say, 'Trip upon Trenchers' or 'There was a Lady all Skin and Bone'.

So I have included plenty of poems about love and death, and many where, as Janet Adam Smith says in the introduction to her excellent *Faber Book of Children's Verse*, understanding will grow with the reader. I have kept most entries short, and have not hesitated to take extracts from longer works. Some will be well-known, others less so; one or two have never to my knowledge been reprinted. I have added a few notes at the end, giving the sources where these are not obvious, and sometimes adding a brief explanation of the historical background or the allusions.

I tried not to look at other anthologies until mine had taken shape, but there were several specialist collections which have been a great help: Iona and Peter Opie's *Oxford Dictionary of Nursery Rhymes* (and also the many old books of rhymes which came to the Bodleian Library with other children's books in the Opie Collection); Francis James Child's *English and Scottish Popular Ballads* (1882); Norman Ault: *Elizabethan Lyrics* (14th edition, 1966);

E. H. Fellowes: *English Madrigal Verse*, revised by F. W. Sternfeld and D. Greer (1967); *A Selection of English Carols* ed. Richard Leighton Greene (1962); *Poems from Black Africa* ed. Langston Hughes (1963); *The Oxford Book of Traditional Verse* ed. Frederick Woods (1979); *The Oxford Book of American Light Verse* ed. William Harmon (1979), and *The New Oxford Book of Eighteenth Century Verse* ed. Roger Lonsdale (1984).

I was sad to come to the end of the work on this collection. I can only hope that readers will find in it a quarter of the pleasure that it has given me.

Oxford, 1994.   Gillian Avery

Rhymes and nonsense

GRAY GOOSE

Gray goose and gander,
   Waft your wings together,
And carry the good king's daughter
   Over the one-strand river.

              ANONYMOUS

THE BOATMAN

Call John the boatman
  Call, call again.
  For loud flows the river
  And fast falls the rain.
John is a good man and sleeps very sound;
His oars are at rest, and his boat is aground.
Fast flows the river so rapid and deep;
The louder you call him, the sounder he'll sleep.

              ANONYMOUS

I HAD A LITTLE CASTLE

I had a little castle upon the seaside,
One half was water, the other was land;
I opened my little castle door, and guess what I found:
  I found a fair lady with a cup in her hand.
  The cup was gold, and filled with wine;
  Drink, fair lady, and thou shalt be mine!

              ANONYMOUS

THE BELLMAN'S SONG

Maids to bed and cover coal;
Let the mouse out of her hole;
Crickets in the chimney sing
Whilst the little bell doth ring:
If fast asleep, who can tell
When the clapper hits the bell?

ANONYMOUS

From Thomas Ravencroft: *Melisma*
1611

THE OWL

Once I was a monarch's daughter,
   And sat on a lady's knee;
But now I am a nightly rover,
   Banished to the ivy tree.
Crying, Hoo, hoo, hoo, hoo, hoo, hoo,
   Hoo, hoo, hoo, my feet are cold,
Pity me, for here you see me
   Persecuted, poor, and old.

ANONYMOUS

A CATCH

Buzz! quoth the Blue-Fly,
Hum! quoth the Bee;
Buzz and hum! they cry
   And so do we.
In his ear! in his nose!
Thus, – do you see?
He eat the Dormouse –
   Else it was he.

BEN JONSON (1572/3–1637)
From *Oberon, the Fairy Prince*

THE MAN IN THE WILDERNESS

The Man in the Wilderness asked of me
'How many blackberries grow in the sea?'
I answered him as I thought good,
'As many red herrings as grow in the wood.'

The Man in the Wilderness asked me why
His hen could swim, and his pig could fly.
I answered him briskly as I thought best,
'Because they were born in a cuckoo's nest.'

The Man in the Wilderness asked me to tell
The sands in the sea and I counted them well.
Says he with a grin, 'And not one more?'
I answered him bravely, 'You go and make sure.'

ANONYMOUS

I'LL BARK AGAINST THE DOG-STAR

I'll bark against the Dog-star,
And crow away the morning;
  I'll chase the moon
  Till it be noon,
And I'll make her leave her horning.

I'll crack the Poles asunder,
  Strange things I will devise on.
I'll beat my brain against Charles's Wain,
  And I'll grasp the round horizon.

I'll search the caves of Slumber,
  And please her in a night-dream;
I'll tumble her into Lawrence's fen,
  And hang myself in a sunbeam.

I'll sail upon a millstone,
  And make the sea-gods wonder,
I'll plunge in the deep, till I wake asleep,
  And I'll tear the rocks in sunder.

              ANONYMOUS

THE MERRY BELLS OF LONDON

Gay go up and gay go down,
To ring the bells of London Town.

Bull's eyes and targets,
Say the bells of St Marg'ret's.

Brickbats and tiles,
Say the bells of St Giles.

Halfpence and farthings,
Say the bells of St Martin's.

Oranges and lemons,
Say the bells of St Clement's.

Pancakes and fritters,
Say the bells of St Peter's.

Two sticks and an apple,
Say the bells at Whitechapel.

Old Father Baldpate,
Say the slow bells at Aldgate.

You owe me ten shillings,
Say the bells of St Helen's.

When will you pay me?
Say the bells at Old Bailey.

When I shall grow rich,
Say the bells at Shoreditch.

Pray, when will that be?
Say the bells at Stepney.

I am sure I don't know,
Says the great bell at Bow.

ANONYMOUS

UPON PAUL'S STEEPLE

Upon Paul's steeple stands a tree
As full of apples as may be;
The little boys of London Town
They run with hooks to pull them down:
And then they run from hedge to hedge,
Until they come to London Bridge.

ANONYMOUS

TRIP UPON TRENCHERS

Trip upon trenchers, and dance upon dishes,
My mother sent me for some barm, some barm;
She bid me tread lightly, and come again quickly,
For fear the young men should do me some harm.
  Yet didn't you see, yet didn't you see,
  What naughty tricks they put upon me:
    They broke my pitcher,
    And spilt the water,
    And huffed my mother,
    And chid her daughter,
  And kissed my sister instead of me.

ANONYMOUS

barm: yeast

A MAN OF WORDS

A man of words and not of deeds
Is like a garden full of weeds;
And when the weeds begin to grow,
It's like a garden full of snow;
And when the snow begins to fall,
It's like a bird upon the wall;
And when the bird away does fly,
It's like an eagle in the sky;
And when the sky begins to roar,
It's like a lion at the door;
And when the door begins to crack,
It's like a stick across your back;
And when your back begins to smart,
It's like a penknife in your heart;
And when your heart begins to bleed,
You're dead, and dead, and dead, indeed.

ANONYMOUS

WHITE BIRD FEATHERLESS

White bird featherless
Flew from Paradise,
Pitched on the castle wall;
Along came Lord Landless,
Took it up handless,
And rode away horseless to the King's white hall.

ANONYMOUS

THE KEY OF THE KINGDOM

This is the key of the kingdom:
In that kingdom is a city,
In that city is a town,
In that town there is a street,
In that street there winds a lane,
In that lane there is a yard,
In that yard there is a house,
In that house there waits a room,
In that room there is a bed,
On that bed there is a basket,
   A basket of flowers.

Flowers in the basket,
Basket on the bed,
Bed in the chamber,
Chamber in the house,
House in the weedy yard,
Yard in the winding lane,
Lane in the broad street,
Street in the high town,
Town in the city,
City in the kingdom:
   This is the key of the kingdom.

ANONYMOUS

THE FROG AND MOUSE

There was a frog liv'd in a well,
   Kitty alone, Kitty alone,
There was a frog liv'd in a well,
   Kitty alone and I.
There was a frog liv'd in a well,
And a farce mouse in a mill,
   Cock me cary, Kitty alone,
   Kitty alone and I.

This frog he would a wooing ride,
      And on a snail he got astride.

He rode till he came to my Lady Mouse hall,
And there he did both knock and call.

Quoth he, 'Miss Mouse, I'm come to thee,
To see if thou can fancy me.'

Quoth she, 'Answer I'll give you none,
Until my Uncle Rat comes home.'

And when her Uncle Rat came home,
'Who's been here since I've been gone?'

'Sir, there's been a worthy gentleman,
That's been here since you've been gone.'

The frog he came whistling through the brook,
And there he met with a dainty duck.

farce: merry

This duck she swallow'd him up with a pluck,
   Kitty alone, Kitty alone.
This duck she swallow'd him up with a pluck,
   Kitty alone and I.
This duck she swallow'd him up with a pluck,
So that's an end of my history book,
  Cock me cary, Kitty alone,
  Kitty alone and I.

ANONYMOUS

THREE YOUNG RATS

Three young rats with black felt hats,
Three young ducks with white straw flats,
Three young dogs with curling tails,
Three young cats with demi-veils,
Went out to walk with two young pigs
In satin vests and sorrel wigs.
But suddenly it chanced to rain
And so they all went home again.

ANONYMOUS

THE FOX'S RAID

A fox jumped up one winter's night
And begged the moon to give him light,
For he'd many miles to trot that night
Before he reached his den O!
    Den O! Den O!
For he'd many miles to trot that night
Before he reached his den O!

The first place he came to was a farmer's yard,
Where the ducks and the geese declared it hard
That their nerves should be shaken and their rest be marred
By a visit from Mr Fox O!
    Fox O! Fox O!
That their nerves should be shaken and their rest so marred
By a visit from Mr Fox O!

He took the grey goose by the neck,
And swung him right across his back;
They grey goose cried out, Quack, quack, quack,
With his legs hanging dangling down O!
    Down O! Down O!
The grey goose cried out, Quack, quack, quack,
With his legs hanging dangling down O!

Old Mother Slipper Slopper jumped out of bed,
And out of the window she popped her head;
Oh! John, John, John, the grey goose is gone,
And the fox is off to his den O!
    Den O! Den O!
Oh! John, John, John, the grey goose is gone,
And the fox is off to his den O!

John ran up to the top of the hill,
And blew his whistle loud and shrill;
Said the fox, That is very pretty music; still —
I'd rather be in my den O!
    Den O! Den O!
Said the fox, That is very pretty music; still —
I'd rather be in my den O!

The fox went back to his hungry den,
And his dear little foxes, eight, nine, ten;
Quoth they, good daddy, you must go there again,
If you bring such good cheer from the farm O!
    Farm O! Farm O!
Quoth they, Good daddy, you must go there again,
If you bring such good cheer from the farm O!

The fox and his wife, without any strife,
Said they never ate a better goose in all their life;
They did very well without fork or knife,
And the little ones picked the bones O!
    Bones O! Bones O!
They did very well without fork or knife,
And the little ones picked the bones O!

ANONYMOUS

THE DRUNKARD AND THE PIG

It was early last December,
As near as I remember,
I was walking down the street in tipsy pride;

No one was I disturbing
As I lay down by the kerbing,
And a pig came up and lay down by my side.
As I lay there in the gutter
Thinking thoughts I shall not utter,
A lady passing by was heard to say:
'You can tell a man who boozes
By the company he chooses.'
And the pig got up and slowly walked away.

ANONYMOUS

BLACK SHEEP

There was an old man of Khartoum
Who kept two black sheep in his room.
  'They remind me,' he said
  'Of some friends who are dead,
But I can never remember of whom.'

ANONYMOUS

SISTERS

If only I hadn't had sisters
How much more romantic I would be.
But my sisters were such little blisters
That all women are sisters to me.

ANONYMOUS

THERE WAS A MONKEY

There was a monkey climbed a tree,
When he fell down, then down fell he.

There was a crow sat on a stone,
When he was gone, then there was none.

There was an old wife did eat an apple,
When she ate two, she ate a couple.

There was a horse going to the mill,
When he went on, he stood not still.

There was a butcher cut his thumb,
When it did bleed, then blood did come.

There was a lackey ran a race,
When he ran fast, he ran apace.

There was a cobbler clouting shoon,
When they were mended, they were done.

There was a navy went to Spain,
When it returned it came again.

ANONYMOUS

A TRAGIC STORY

There liv'd a sage in days of yore,
And he a handsome pigtail wore,
But wonder'd much and sorrow'd more,
Because it hung behind him.

He mus'd upon this curious case,
And swore he'd change the pigtail's place,
And have it dangling at his face,
Not dangling there behind him.

Says he, 'The mystery I've found, –
I'll turn me round.' –
He turn'd him round,
But still it hung behind him.

Then round and round, and out and in,
All day the puzzled sage did spin;
In vain – it matter'd not a pin,
The pigtail hung behind him.

And right and left, and round about,
And up and down, and in and out he turn'd,
But still the pigtail stout
Hung steadily behind him.

And though his efforts never slack,
And though he twist, and twirl, and tack,
Alas! still faithful to his back,
The pigtail hangs behind him.

WILLIAM MAKEPEACE
THACKERAY (1811–63)

THE THREE BADGERS

There be three Badgers on a mossy stone,
    Beside a dark and covered way:
Each dreams himself a monarch on his throne,
    And so they stay and stay –
Though their old Father languishes alone,
    They stay, and stay, and stay.

There be three Herrings loitering around,
    Longing to share that mossy seat:
Each Herring tries to sing what she has found
    That makes Life seem so sweet.
Thus, with a grating and uncertain sound,
    They bleat, and bleat, and bleat.

The Mother-Herring, on the salt sea-wave,
    Sought vainly for her absent ones:
The Father-Badger, writhing in a cave,
    Shrieked out, 'Return, my sons!
You shall have buns,' he shrieked, 'if you'll behave!
    Yea, buns, and buns, and buns!'

'I fear,' said she, 'your sons have gone astray?
    My daughters left me while I slept.'
'Yes'm,' the Badger said: 'it's as you say.
    They should be better kept.'
Thus the poor parents talked the time away,
    And wept, and wept, and wept.

THE HERRINGS' SONG

'Oh, dear beyond our dearest dreams,
    Fairer than all that fairest seems!
To feast the rosy hours away,
To revel in a roundelay!
      How blest would be
      A life so free –
Ipwergis-Pudding to consume,
And drink the subtle Azzigoom!'

The Badgers did not care to talk to Fish:
    They did not dote on Herrings' songs:
They never had experienced the dish
    To which that name belongs:
'And oh, to pinch their tails' (this was their wish)
    'With tongs, yea, tongs, and tongs!'

'And are not these the Fish,' the Eldest sighed,
    'Whose Mother dwells beneath the foam?'
'They *are* the Fish!' the Second one replied.
    'And they have left their home!'
'Oh wicked fish,' the Youngest Badger cried,
    'To roam, yea, roam, and roam!'

Gently the Badgers trotted to the shore –
    The sandy shore that fringed the bay:
Each in his mouth a living Herring bore –
    Those aged ones waxed gay:
Clear rang their voices through the ocean's roar,
    'Hooray, hooray, hooray!'

LEWIS CARROLL (1832–98)

From *Sylvie and Bruno*

THE TABLE AND THE CHAIR

Said the Table to the Chair,
'You can hardly be aware,
How I suffer from the heat,
And from chilblains on my feet!
If we took a little walk,
We might have a little talk!
Pray let us take the air!'
Said the Table to the Chair.

Said the Chair unto the Table,
'Now you *know* we are not able!
How foolishly you talk,
When you know we *cannot* walk!'
Said the Table, with a sigh,
'It can do no harm to try,
I've as many legs as you,
Why can't we walk on two?'

So they both went slowly down,
And walked about the town
With a cheerful bumpy sound,
As they toddled round and round,
And everybody cried,
As they hastened to their side,
'See! the Table and the Chair
Have come out to take the air!'

But in going down an alley,
To a castle in a valley,
They completely lost their way,
And wandered all the day,
Till, to see them safely back,
They paid a Ducky-quack,
And a Beetle, and a Mouse,
Who took them to their house.

Then they whispered to each other,
'O delightful little brother!
What a lovely walk we've taken!
Let us dine on Beans and Bacon!'
So the Ducky, and the leetle
Browny-Mousy and the Beetle
Dined, and danced upon their heads
Till they toddled to their beds.

EDWARD LEAR (1812–88)

THE OWL AND THE EEL AND THE WARMING-PAN

The Owl and the Eel and the Warming-pan,
They went to call on the soap-fat man.
The soap-fat man he was not within:
He'd gone for a ride on his rolling-pin.
So they all came back by way of the town,
And turned the meeting-house upside down.

LAURA RICHARDS

(1850–1943)

CALICO PIE

Calico Pie,
The little Birds fly
Down to the calico tree,
Their wings were blue,
And they sang 'Tilly-loo!'
Till away they flew,–
And they never came back to me!
They never came back!
They never came back!
They never came back to me!

Calico Jam,
The little Fish swam,
Over the syllabub sea,
He took off his hat
To the Sole and the Sprat,
And the Willeby-wat,–
But he never came back to me!
He never came back!
He never came back!
He never came back to me!

Calico Ban,
The little Mice ran,
To be ready in time for tea,
Flippity flup,
They drank it all up,
And danced in the cup, –
But they never came back to me!
They never came back!
They never came back!
They never came back to me!

    Calico Drum,
   The Grasshoppers come,
  The Butterfly, Beetle, and Bee,
    Over the ground,
    Around and round,
   With a hop and a bound, –
But they never came back!
   They never came back!
   They never came back!
They never came back to me!

EDWARD LEAR (1812–88)

CRAQUEODOOM

The Crankadox leaned o'er the edge of the moon
 And wistfully gazed on the sea
Where the Gryxabodill madly whistled a tune
 To the air of 'Ti-fol-de-ding-dee.'
The quavering shriek of the Fly-up-the-creek
 Was fitfully wafted afar
To the Queen of the Wunks as she powdered her cheek
 With the pulverized rays of a star.

The Gool closed his ear on the voice of the Grig,
 And his heart it grew heavy as lead
As he marked the Baldekin adjusting his wing
 On the opposite side of his head,
And the air it grew chill as the Gryxabodill
 Raised his dank, dripping fins to the skies,
And plead with the Plunk for the use of her bill
 To pick the tears out of his eyes.

The ghost of the Zhack flitted by in a trance,
    And the Squidjum hid under a tub
As he heard the loud hooves of the Hooken advance
    With a rub-a-dub - dub a dub - dub!
And the Crankadox cried, as he laid down and died,
    'My fate there is none to bewail,'
While the Queen of the Wunks drifted over the tide
    With a long piece of crape to her tail.

JAMES WHITCOMB RILEY
(1849–1916)

THE FOOLISH BOY

When I was a little boy, I lived by myself,
And all the bread and cheese I got I laid them on the shelf.

The rats and the mice they gave me such a life,
I had to go to London to get me a wife.

The roads were so long, and the streets were so narrow,
I had to bring her home on an old wheelbarrow.

My foot slipped and I got a fall,
Down went wheelbarrow, wife and all.

I swapped my wheelbarrow and got me a horse,
And then I rode from cross to cross.

I swapped my horse and got me a mare,
And then I rode from fair to fair.

I swapped my mare and got me a cow,
And in that trade I just learned how.

I swapped my cow and got me a calf,
And in that trade I just lost half.

I swapped my calf and got me a mule,
And then I rode like a doggone fool.

I swapped my mule and got me a sheep,
And then I rode myself to sleep.

I swapped my sheep and got me a hen,
O what a pretty thing I had then.

I swapped my hen and got me a rat,
Set it on the haystack to run the cat.

I swapped my rat and got me a mole,
And the doggone thing went straight to its hole.

ANONYMOUS

I SOMETIMES THINK

I sometimes think I'd rather crow,
And be a rooster,
Than to roost and be a crow,
   But I don't know.

The rooster he can roost also,
Which don't seem fair,
'Cos crows can't crow
   Still, I don't know.

Crows should be glad of one thing, though.
Nobody thinks of eating crow.
The rooster, he is good enough
For anyone, unless he's tough.

There's lots of tough old roosters, though,
And anyway a crow can't crow.
So maybe roosters stand more show.
It looks that way.
   But I don't know.

                             ANONYMOUS

THE COMMON CORMORANT

The common cormorant or shag
Lays eggs inside a paper bag.
The reason you will see no doubt
It is to keep the lightning out.
But what those unobservant birds
Have never noticed is that herds
Of wandering bears may come with buns
And steal the bags to hold the crumbs.

                             ANONYMOUS

TWO OLD CROWS

Two old crows sat on a fence rail,
Two old crows sat on a fence rail,
Talking of effect and cause,
Of weeds and flowers,
And nature's laws.
One of them muttered, one of them stuttered.
Each of them thought far more than he uttered.
One crow asked the other crow a riddle.
One crow asked the other crow a riddle.
The muttering crow
Asked the stuttering crow,
'Why does a bee have a sword to his fiddle?
Why does a bee have a sword to his fiddle?'
'Bee-cause,' said the other crow,
'Bee-cause,
B B B B B B B B B B B B B B B-cause.'
Just then a bee flew close to their rail:–
'Buzzzzzzzzzzzzzzzzzz zzzzzzzz zzzzzzzzzzzzz
   ZZZZZZZZ.'
And those two black crows
Turned pale,
And away those crows did sail.
Why?
B B B B B B B B B B B B B B B-cause.
B B B B B B B B B B B B B B B-cause.
'Buzzzzzzzzzzzzzzzzzz zzzzzzz zzzzzzzzzzzzz
   ZZZZZZZZ.'

                              VACHEL LINDSAY
                                (1879–1931)

CLEMENTINE

In a cavern in a canyon, excavating for a mine,
Dwelt a miner, forty-niner, and his daughter, Clementine.
  Oh, my darling, oh, my darling, oh, my darling Clementine,
  You are lost and gone forever, dreadful sorry, Clementine.

Light she was and like a fairy, and her shoes were number nine,
Herring boxes without topses, sandals were for Clementine.

Drove her ducklings to the water, every morning just at nine,
Hit her foot against a splinter, fell into the foaming brine.

Ruby lips above the water, blowing bubbles soft and fine,
Alas, for me! I was no swimmer, so I lost my Clementine.

In a churchyard, near the canyon, where the myrtle doth entwine,
There grow roses and other posies fertilized by Clementine.

Then the miner, forty-niner, soon began to droop and pine,
Thought he ought to join his daughter, now he's with his Clementine.

In my dreams she still doth haunt me, robed in garments soaked in brine,
Though in life I used to kiss her, now she's dead I draw the line.
  Oh, my darling, oh, my darling, oh, my darling Clementine,
  You are lost and gone forever, dreadful sorry, Clementine.

                            ANONYMOUS

forty-niner: migrant to California in the gold rush of 1849

THE EDDYSTONE LIGHT

Me father was the keeper of the Eddystone Light,
He lay with a mermaid one fine night;
And of the match came children three –
A porgy, and a dolphin and the other was me.
   Jolly stories, jolly told
   When the winds is bleak and the nights is cold;
   No such life can be led on the shore
   As is had on the rocks by the ocean's roar.

When I was but a boyish chip,
They put me in charge of the old lightship;
I trimmed the lamps and I filled 'em with oil,
And I played Seven-up accordin' to Hoyle.

One evenin' as I was a-trimming' the glim
An' singin' a verse of the evenin' hymn,
I see by the light of me binnacle lamp
Me kind old father lookin' jolly and damp;
An' a voice from the starboard shouted 'Ahoy!'
An' there was me gran'mother sittin' on a buoy –
Meanin' a buoy for ships what sail
An' not a boy what's a juvenile male.
   Jolly stories, jolly told
   When the winds is bleak and the nights is cold;
   No such life can be led on the shore
   As is had on the rocks by the ocean's roar.

                                     ANONYMOUS

The year and its seasons

IT'S NEVER FAIR WEATHER

I do not like the winter wind
That whistles from the North.
My upper teeth and those beneath,
They jitter back and forth.
Oh some are hanged, and some are skinned,
And others face the winter wind.

I do not like the summer sun
That scorches the horizon.
Though some delight in Fahrenheit,
To me it's deadly pizen.
I think that life would be more fun
Without the simmering summer sun.

I do not like the signs of spring,
The fever and the chills,
The icy mud, the puny bud,
The frozen daffodils.
Let other poets gayly sing;
I do not like the signs of spring.

I do not like the foggy fall
That strips the maples bare;
The radiator's mating call,
The dank, rheumatic air.
I fear that taken all in all,
I do not like the foggy fall.

The winter sun, of course, is kind,
And summer wind's a savior,
And I'll merrily sing of fall and spring
When they're on their good behavior.
But otherwise I see no reason
To speak in praise of any season.

OGDEN NASH (1902–71)

A NEW YEAR CAROL

Here we bring you new water from the well so clear,
For to worship God with this happy New Year.
Sing levy dew, the water and the wine;
The seven bright gold wires
And the bugles that do shine.

Sing reign of Fair Maid, with gold upon her toe,
Open you the West Door and turn the Old Year go.
Sing levy dew, the water and the wine;
The seven bright gold wires
And the bugles that do shine.

Sing reign of Fair Maid, with gold upon her chin,
Open you the East Door and let the New Year in.
Sing levy dew, the water and the wine;
The seven bright gold wires
And the bugles that do shine.

ANONYMOUS

HOT CAKE

Winter has come; fierce is the cold;
In the sharp morning air new-risen we meet.
Rheum freezes in the nose;
Frost hangs about the chin.
For hollow bellies, for chattering teeth and shivering knees
What better than hot cake?
Soft as the down of spring,
Whiter than autumn floss!
Dense and swift the steam
Rises, swells and spreads,
Fragrance flies through the air,
Is scattered far and wide,
Steals down along the wind and wets
The covetous mouth of passer-by.
Servants and grooms
Throw sidelong glances, munch the empty air.
They lick their lips who serve;
While lines of envious lackeys by the wall
Stand dryly swallowing.

From a poem by SHU HSI (c. A.D. 265–306)

trans. Arthur Waley

WINTER

When icicles hang by the wall,
    And Dick the shepherd blows his nail,
And Tom bears logs into the hall,
    And milk comes frozen home in pail;

When blood is nipp'd, and ways be foul,
Then nightly sings the staring owl,
   Tu-who;
Tu-whit, tu-who – a merry note,
While greasy Joan doth keel the pot.

When all aloud the wind doth blow,
   And coughing drowns the parson's saw,
And birds sit brooding in the snow,
   And Marian's nose looks red and raw,
When roasted crabs hiss in the bowl,
Then nightly sings the staring owl,
   Tu-who,
Tu-whit, tu-who – a merry note,
While greasy Joan doth keel the pot.

WILLIAM SHAKESPEARE (1564–1616)
Love's Labour's Lost, V ii

saw: sermon

From THE EVE OF ST AGNES

St Agnes' Eve – Ah, bitter chill it was!
The owl, for all his feathers, was a-cold;
The hare limp'd trembling through the frozen grass,
And silent was the flock in woolly fold:
Numb were the Beadsman's fingers, while he told
His rosary, and while his frosted breath,
Like pious incense from a censer old,
Seem'd taking flight for heaven, without a death,
Past the sweet Virgin's picture, while his prayer he saith.

    His prayer he saith, this patient, holy man;
    Then takes his lamp, and riseth from his knees,
    And back returneth, meagre, barefoot, wan,
    Along the chapel aisle by slow degrees:
    The sculptur'd dead, on each side, seem to freeze,
    Emprison'd in black, purgatorial rails:
    Knights, ladies, praying in dumb orat'ries,
    He passeth by; and his weak spirit fails
To think how they may ache in icy hoods and mails.

                    JOHN KEATS (1795–1821)

LONDON SNOW

When men were all asleep the snow came flying,
In large white flakes falling on the city brown,
Stealthily and perpetually settling and loosely lying,
    Hushing the latest traffic of the drowsy town;
Deadening, muffling, stifling its murmurs failing;
Lazily and incessantly floating down and down;
    Silently sifting and veiling road, roof and railing;
Hiding difference, making unevenness even,
Into angles and crevices softly drifting and sailing.
    All night it fell, and when full inches seven
It lay in the depth of its uncompacted lightness,
The clouds blew off from a high and frosty heaven;
    And all woke earlier for the unaccustomed brightness
Of the winter dawning, the strange unheavenly glare:
The eye marvelled – marvelled at the dazzling whiteness;
    The ear hearkened to the stillness of the solemn air;
No sound of wheel rumbling nor of foot falling,

And the busy morning cries came thin and spare.
    Then boys I heard, as they went to school, calling,
They gathered up the crystal manna to freeze
Their tongues with tasting, their hands with snowballing;
    Or rioted in a drift, plunging up to the knees;
Or peering up from under the white-mossed wonder,
'O look at the trees!' they cried, 'O look at the trees!'
    With lessened load a few carts creak and blunder,
Following along the white deserted way,
A country company long dispersed asunder:
    When now already, the sun, in pale display
Standing by Paul's high dome, spread forth below
His sparkling beams, and awoke the stir of day.
    For now doors open, and war is waged with the snow;
And trains of sombre men, past tale of number,
Tread long brown paths, as toward their toil they go:
    But even for them awhile no cares encumber
Their minds diverted; the daily word is unspoken,
The daily thoughts of labour and sorrow slumber
At the sight of the beauty that greets them, for the charm they
                            have broken.

ROBERT BRIDGES (1844–1930)

Two triolets
BIRDS AT WINTER NIGHTFALL

Around the house the flakes fly faster,
And all the berries now are gone
From holly and cotonea-aster
Around the house. The flakes fly! – faster
Shutting indoors that crumb-outcaster
We used to see upon the lawn
Around the house. The flakes fly faster,
And all the berries now are gone!

WINTER IN DURNOVER FIELD

SCENE. – A wide stretch of fallow ground recently sown with wheat, and frozen to iron hardness. Three large birds walking about thereon, and wistfully eying the surface. Wind keen from north-east: sky a dull grey.

Rook.   Throughout the field I find no grain;
           The cruel frost encrusts the cornland!
Starling. Aye: patient pecking now is vain
           Throughout the field, I find . . .
Rook.   no grain!
Pigeon. Nor will be, comrade, till it rain,
           Or genial thawings loose the lorn land
           Throughout the field.
Rook.   I find no grain:
           The cruel frost encrusts the cornland.

THOMAS HARDY (1840–1928)

STAR-TALK

'Are you awake, Gemelli,
  This frosty night?'
'We'll be awake till reveillé,
Which is Sunrise,' say the Gemelli,
'It's no good trying to go to sleep:
If there's wine to be got we'll drink it deep,
  But sleep is gone for to-night,
  But sleep is gone for to-night.'

'Are you cold too, poor Pleiads,
  This frosty night?'
'Yes, and so are the Hyads:
See us cuddle and hug,' said the Pleiads,
'All six in a ring; it keeps us warm:
We huddle together like birds in a storm:
  It's bitter weather to-night,
  It's bitter weather to-night.'

'What do you hunt, Orion,
  This starry night?'
'The Ram, the Bull and the Lion,
And the Great Bear,' says Orion,
'With my starry quiver and beautiful belt
I am trying to find a good thick pelt
  To warm my shoulders to-night,
  To warm my shoulders to-night.'

'Did you hear that, Great She-bear,
  This frosty night?'
'Yes, he's talking of stripping me bare
Of my own big fur,' says the She-bear,

'I'm afraid of the man and his terrible arrow;
The thought of it chills my bones to the marrow,
   And the frost so cruel to-night!
   And the frost so cruel to-night!'

'How is your trade, Aquarius,
   This frosty night?'
'Complaints is many and various
And my feet are cold,' says Aquarius,
'There's Venus objects to Dolphin-scales,
And Mars to Crab-spawn found in my pails,
   And the pump has frozen to-night,
   And the pump has frozen to-night.'

              ROBERT GRAVES (1895–1985)

THE SCARECROW

All winter through I bow my head
   Beneath the driving rain;
The North Wind powders me with snow
   And blows me black again;
At midnight in a maze of stars
   I flame with glittering rime,
And stand, above the stubble, stiff
   As mail at morning-prime.
But when that child, called Spring, and all
   His host of children, come,
Scattering their buds and dew upon
   These acres of my home,
Some rapture in my rags awakes;
   I lift void eyes and scan

The skies for crows, those ravening foes
    Of my strange master, Man.
I watch him striding lank behind
    His clashing team, and know
Soon will the wheat swish body high
    Where once lay sterile snow;
Soon shall I gaze across a sea
    Of sun-begotten grain,
Which my unflinching watch hath sealed
    For harvest once again.

            WALTER DE LA MARE (1873–1956)

CEREMONIES FOR CANDLEMASS EVE

Down with the rosemary and bays,
    Down with the mistletoe;
Instead of holly, now upraise
    The greener box, for show.

The holly hitherto did sway;
    Let box now domineer;
Until the dancing Easter-day,
    Or Easter's eve appear.

Then youthful box which now hath grace,
    Your houses to renew,
Grown old, surrender must his place,
    Unto the crispèd yew.

When yew is out, then birch comes in,
    And many flowers beside;
Both of a fresh, and fragrant kin
    To honour Whitsuntide.
Green bushes then, and sweetest bents,
    With cooler oaken boughs;
Come in for comely ornaments,
    To re-adorn the house.
Thus times do shift; each thing his turn does hold;
New things succeed, as former things grow old.

ROBERT HERRICK (1591–1674)

AT CANDLEMAS

'If Candlemas is fine and clear
There'll be two winters in that year';

But all the day the drumming sun
Brazened it out that spring had come,

And the tall elder on the scene
Unfolded the first leaves of green.

But when another morning came
With frost, as Candlemas with flame,

The sky was steel, there was no sun,
And the elder leaves were dead and gone.

Out of a cold and crusted eye
The stiff pond stared up at the sky,

And on the scarcely breathing earth
A killing wind fell from the north;

But still within the elder tree
The strong sap rose, though none could see.

CHARLES CAUSLEY (1917–　)

WHEN MARCH BLOWS

When March blows, and Monday's linen is shown
On the gooseberry bushes, and the worried washer alone
Fights at the soaked stuff, meres and the rutted pools
Mirror the wool-pack clouds, and shine clearer than jewels.

And the children throw stones in them, spoil mirror and clouds.
And the worry of washing over, the worry of foods
Brings tea-time; March quietens as the trouble dies.
The washing is brought in under wind-swept clear infinite skies.

IVOR GURNEY (1890–1937)

SPRING

When daisies pied and violets blue
    And lady-smocks all silver-white
  And cuckoo-buds of yellow hue
    Do paint the meadows with delight,

The cuckoo then, on every tree,
Mocks married men; for thus sings he,
   Cuckoo;
Cuckoo, cuckoo: O, word of fear,
Unpleasing to a married ear!

When shepherds pipe on oaten straws,
   And merry larks are ploughmen's clocks,
When turtles tread, and rooks, and daws,
   And maidens bleach their summer smocks,
The cuckoo then, on every tree,
Mocks married men; for thus sings he,
   Cuckoo;
Cuckoo, cuckoo: O, word of fear,
Unpleasing to a married ear!

WILLIAM SHAKESPEARE (1564–1616)
Love's Labour's Lost, V ii

WEATHERS

I

This is the weather the cuckoo likes,
   And so do I;
When showers betumble the chestnut spikes,
   And nestlings fly;
And the little brown nightingale bills his best,
And they sit outside at 'The Travellers' Rest',
And maids come forth sprig-muslin drest,
And citizens dream of the south and west,
   And so do I.

II

This is the weather the shepherd shuns,
    And so do I;
When beeches drip in browns and duns,
    And thresh, and ply;
And hill-hid tides throb, throe on throe,
And meadow rivulets overflow,
And drops on gate-bars hang in a row,
And rooks in families homeward go,
    And so do I.

THOMAS HARDY (1840–1928)

SPRING

Pale sunbeams gleam
That nurture a few flowers,
Pile wort and daisy and a sprig o' green
On white thorn bushes
In the leaf strewn hedge.

These harbingers
Tell spring is coming fast,
And these the schoolboy marks
And wastes an hour from school
Agen the old pasture hedge,

Cropping the daisy
And the pile wort flowers.
Pleased with the spring and all he looks upon
He opes his spelling book
And hides her blossoms there.

Shadows fall dark
Like black in the pale sun
And lie the bleak day long,
Like black stock under hedges
And bare wind-rocked trees.

'Tis chill but pleasant
In the hedge bottom lined
With brown sear leaves the last
Year littered there and left,
Mopes the hedge sparrow

With trembling wings and cheeps
Its welcome to pale sunbeams
Creeping through. And further on,
Made of green moss,
The nest and green blue eggs are seen.

All token spring and every day
Green and more green hedges and close
And everywhere appears.
Still 'tis but March
But still that March is spring.

JOHN CLARE (1793–1864)

MIRTH

If you are merry sing away,
    And touch the organs sweet;
This is the Lord's triumphant day,
Ye children in the galleries gay,
    Shout from each goodly seat.

It shall be May tomorrow's morn,
   A-field then let us run,
And deck us in the blooming thorn,
Soon as the cock begins to warn,
   And long before the sun.

I give the praise to Christ alone,
   My pinks already show;
And my streaked roses fully blown,
The sweetness of the Lord make known,
   And to his glory grow.

Ye little prattlers that repair
   For cowslips in the mead,
Of these exulting colts beware,
But blithe security is there,
   Where skipping lambkins feed.

With white and crimson laughs the sky,
   With birds the hedgerows ring;
To give the praise to God most high,
And all the sulky fiends defy,
   Is a most joyful thing.

        CHRISTOPHER SMART (1722–71)

A SUMMER'S DAY

Oh, many a time have I, a five year's child,
A naked boy, in one delightful rill,
A little mill-race severed from his stream,
Made one long bathing of a summer's day;
Basked in the sun, and plunged and basked again
Alternate, all a summer's day, or coursed

Over the sandy fields, leaping through groves
Of yellow groundsel; or when crag and hill,
The woods and distant Skiddaw's lofty height,
Were bronzed with a deep radiance, stood alone
Beneath the sky, as if I had been born
On Indian plains, and from my mother's hut
Had run abroad in wantonness, to sport
A naked savage, in the thunder shower.

WILLIAM WORDSWORTH (1770–1850)

From *The Prelude*, Book I

ANSWER JULY

Answer July –
Where is the Bee –
Where is the Blush –
Where is the Hay?

Ah, said July –
Where is the Seed –
Where is the Bud –
Where is the May –
Answer Thee – Me –

Nay – said the May –
Show me the Snow –
Show me the Bells –
Show me the Jay!

Quibbled the Jay –
Where be the Maize –
Where be the Haze –
Where be the Bur?
Here – said the Year.

EMILY DICKINSON (1830–86)

THE OVEN BIRD

There is a singer everyone has heard,
Loud, a mid-summer and a mid-wood bird,
Who makes the solid tree trunks sound again.
He says that leaves are old and that for flowers
Mid-summer is to spring as one to ten.
He says the early petal-fall is past
Where pear and cherry bloom went down in showers
On sunny days a moment overcast;
And comes that other fall we name the fall.
He says the highway dust is over all.
The bird would cease and be as other birds
But that he knows in singing not to sing.
The question that he frames in all but words
Is what to make of a diminished thing.

ROBERT FROST (1874–1963)

SATIRE ON PAYING CALLS IN AUGUST

When I was young, throughout the hot season
There were no carriages driving about the roads.
People shut their door and lay down in the cool;
Or if they went out, it was not to pay calls.
Nowadays – ill-bred, ignorant fellows,
When they feel the heat, make for a friend's house.
The unfortunate host when he hears someone coming
Scowls and frowns, but can think of no escape.
'There's nothing for it but to rise and go to the door.'
And in his comfortable seat he groans and sighs.
The conversation does not end quickly;
Prattling and babbling, what a lot he says!
Only when one is almost dead with fatigue
He asks at last if one isn't finding him tiring.
(One's arm is almost in half with continual fanning;
The sweat is pouring down one's neck in streams.)
Do not say that this is a small matter;
I consider the practice a blot on our social life.
I therefore caution all wise men
That August visitors should not be admitted.

CH'ENG HSAIO (c. A.D. 220–64)

trans. Arthur Waley

BLACKBERRY-PICKING

Late August, given heavy rain and sun
For a full week, the blackberries would ripen.
At first, just one, a glossy purple clot
Among others, red, green, hard as a knot.
You ate the first one and its flesh was sweet
Like thickened wine: summer's blood was in it
Leaving stains upon the tongue and lust for
Picking. Then red ones inked up and that hunger
Sent us out with milk-cans, pea-tins, jam-pots
Where briars scratched and wet grass bleached our boots.
Round hayfields, cornfields and potato-drills
We trekked and picked until the cans were full,
Until the tinkling bottoms had been covered
With green ones, and on top big dark blobs burned
Like a plate of eyes. Our hands were peppered
With thorn pricks, our palms sticky as Bluebeard's.

We hoarded the fresh berries in the byre.
But when the bath was filled we found a fur,
A rat-grey fungus, glutting on our cache.
The juice was stinking too. Once off the bush
The fruit fermented, the sweet flesh would turn sour.
I always felt like crying. It wasn't fair
That all the lovely canfuls smelt of rot.
Each year I hoped they'd keep, knew they would not.

SEAMUS HEANEY (1939–)

THE WIND BEGAN TO ROCK THE GRASS

The wind began to rock the grass
With threatening tunes and low –
He threw a menace at the earth –
A menace at the sky.

The leaves unhooked themselves from trees –
And started all abroad
The dust did scoop itself like hands
And threw away the road.

The wagons quickened on the streets
The thunder hurried slow –
The lightning showed a yellow beak
And then a livid claw.

The birds put up the bars to nests –
The cattle fled to barns –
There came one drop of giant rain
And then as if the hands

That held the dams had parted hold
The waters wrecked the sky
But overlooked my father's house –
Just quartering a tree.

      EMILY DICKINSON (1830–86)

TO AUTUMN

Season of mists and mellow fruitfulness!
   Close bosom-friend of the maturing sun;
Conspiring with him how to load and bless
   With fruit the vines that round the thatch-eaves run;
To bend with apples the moss'd cottage-trees,
   And fill all fruit with ripeness to the core;
     To swell the gourd, and plump the hazel shells
With a sweet kernel; to set budding more,
And still more, later flowers for the bees,
Until they think warm days will never cease,
   For Summer has o'er-brimmed their clammy cells.

Who hath not seen thee oft amid thy store?
   Sometimes whoever seeks abroad may find
Thee sitting careless on a granary floor,
   Thy hair soft-lifted by the winnowing wind,
Or on a half-reap'd furrow sound asleep,
   Drowsed with the fume of poppies, while thy hook
     Spares the next swath and all its twinèd flowers;
And sometimes like a gleaner thou dost keep
   Steady thy laden head across a brook;
   Or by a cider-press, with patient look,
     Thou watchest the last oozings hours by hours.

Where are the songs of Spring? Ay, where are they?
   Think not of them, thou hast thy music too, –
While barrèd clouds bloom the soft-dying day,
   And touch the stubble-plains with rosy hue;
Then in a wailful choir the small gnats mourn
   Among the river sallows, borne aloft
     Or sinking as the light wind lives or dies;
And full-grown lambs loud bleat from hilly bourn;

> Hedge-crickets sing; and now with treble soft
> The redbreast whistles from a garden-croft;
> And gathering swallows twitter in the skies.

JOHN KEATS (1795–1821)

THE HARVEST MOON

The flame-red moon, the harvest moon,
Rolls along the hills, gently bouncing,
A vast balloon
Till it takes off, and sinks upward
To lie in the bottom of the sky, like a gold doubloon.

The harvest moon has come
Booming softly through heaven, like a bassoon.
And earth replies all night, like a deep drum.

So people can't sleep,
So they go out, where elms and oak trees keep
A kneeling vigil, in a religious hush.
The harvest moon has come!

And all the moonlit cows and all the sheep
Stare up at her petrified, while she swells,
Filling heaven, as if red hot, and sailing
Closer and closer like the end of the world.

Till the gold fields of stiff wheat
Cry 'We are ripe, reap us!' and the rivers
Sweat from the melting hills.

TED HUGHES (1930–   )

MUSHROOMS

Overnight, very
Whitely, discreetly,
Very quietly

Our toes, our noses
Take hold on the loam,
Acquire the air.

Nobody sees us,
Stops us, betrays us;
The small grains make room.

Soft fists insist on
Heaving the needles,
The leafy bedding,

Even the paving.
Our hammers, our rams,
Earless and eyeless,

Perfectly voiceless,
Widen the crannies,
Shoulder through holes. We

Diet on water,
On crumbs of shadow,
Bland-mannered, asking

Little or nothing.
So many of us!
So many of us!

We are shelves, we are
Tables, we are meek,
We are edible,

Nudgers and shovers
In spite of ourselves,
Our kind multiplies;

We shall by morning
Inherit the earth.
Our foot's in the door.

SYLVIA PLATH (1932–63)

HARVEST HYMN

We spray the fields and scatter
   The poison on the ground
So that no wicked wild flowers
   Upon our farm be found.
We like whatever helps us
   To line our purse with pence;
The twenty-four hour broiler-house
   And neat electric fence.

   All concrete sheds around us
      And Jaguars in the yard,
   The telly lounge and deep-freeze
      Are ours from working hard.

We fire the fields for harvest,
　　The hedges swell the flame,
The oak trees and the cottages
　　From which our fathers came.
We give no compensation,
　　The earth is ours today,
And if we lose on arable,
　　Then bungalows will pay.

　　All concrete sheds around us
　　And Jaguars in the yard,
　　The telly lounge and deep-freeze
　　Are ours from working hard.

　　　　　　　　SIR JOHN BETJEMAN (1906–84)

THE LONG AND LONELY WINTER

Summer comes October, the green becomes the brown,
The leaves will all be red and gold before they reach the ground.
Before they reach the ground, my dear, before they reach the ground,
The long and lonely winter will be here.

The early autumn evening was once the afternoon
And now the chill and frosty night it always comes too soon.
It always comes too soon, my dear, it always comes too soon,
The long and lonely winter will be here.

The whitethroat and the swallow are nowhere to be found,
And the redwing is upon the land before you turn around.
Before you turn around, my dear, before you turn around,
The long and lonely winter will be here.

The travellers have left the road so very long and still,
The sun will wait the winter through before he leaves the hill.
Before he leaves the hill, my dear, before he leaves the hill,
The long and lonely winter will be here.

Summer comes October, a season here and gone
And very little time to lose before the day is done,
Before the day is done, my dear, before the day is done,
The long and lonely winter will be here.

DAVE GOULDER (1939-)

AUTUMN

I love the fitful gust that shakes
   The casement all the day,
And from the mossy elm tree takes
   The faded leaf away,
Twirling it by the window pane
With thousand others down the lane.

I love to see the shaking twig
   Dance till the shut of eve,
The sparrow on the cottage rig
   Whose chirp would make believe
That spring was just now flirting by
In summer's lap with flowers to lie.

I love to see the cottage smoke
   Curl upwards through the naked trees;
The pigeons nestled round the cote
   On dull November days like these;
The cock upon the dunghill crowing;
The mill sails on the heath agoing.

The feather from the raven's breast
   Falls on the stubble lea;
The acorns near the old crow's nest
   Fall pattering down the tree.
The grunting pigs that wait for all
Scramble and hurry where they fall.

                JOHN CLARE (1793–1864)

TO-NIGHT THE WINDS BEGIN TO RISE

To-night the winds begin to rise
   And roar from yonder dropping day:
   The last red leaf is whirl'd away,
The rooks are blown about the sky.

The forest crack'd, the waters curl'd,
   The cattle huddled on the lea;
   And wildly dash'd on tower and tree
The sunbeam strikes along the world:

And but for fancies, which aver
   That all thy motions gently pass
   Athwart a plane of molten glass,
I scarce could brook the strain and stir

That makes the barren branches loud;
   And but for fear it is not so,
   The wild unrest that lives in woe
Would dote and pore on yonder cloud

That rises upward always higher,
   And onward drags a labouring breast,
   And topples round the dreary west,
A looming bastion fringed with fire.

               ALFRED,
               LORD TENNYSON (1809–92)

               From *In Memoriam*

ACROSTIC FOR GUY FAWKES NIGHT

G ive me crowding children. A front lawn damp
U nder an angular bejewelled Great Bear.
Y oung hot brothers held to peer through window-bars

F idgeting in vain for rockets due to flare:
A fter altercations round the oily cycle-lamp
W onderful and sudden showers in blackest air,
K ingly gold eclipsing the ineffectual stars.
E very bang expended. One smouldering spark.
S ilence. Smell of sulphur. Reinstated dark.

               FRANCES CORNFORD (1886–1960)

NEW PRINCE, NEW POMP

Behold, a silly tender babe,
   In freezing winter night,
In homely manger trembling lies,
   Alas, a piteous sight!

The inns are full, no man will yield
   This little pilgrim bed;
But forc't he is with silly beasts,
   In crib to shroud his head.

Despise him not for lying there;
   First, what he is enquire:
An orient pearl is often found
   In depth of dirty mire.

Weigh not his crib, his wooden dish,
   Nor beasts that by him feed;
Weigh not his mother's poor attire,
   Nor Joseph's simple weed.

This stable is a prince's court,
   The crib his chair of state;
The beasts are parcel of his pomp,
   The wooden dish his plate.

The persons in that poor attire,
   His royal liveries wear,
The Prince himself is come from Heaven,
   This pomp is prizèd there.

With joy approach, O Christian wight,
   Do homage to thy King;
And highly praise his humble pomp,
   Which he from Heaven doth bring.

                ROBERT SOUTHWELL (?1561–1595)

CEREMONIES FOR CHRISTMAS

   Come, bring with a noise,
    My merry merry boys,
The Christmas log to the firing;
   While my good Dame, she
    Bids ye all be free;
And drink to your heart's desiring.

   With the last year's brand
    Light the new block, and
For good success in his spending,
   On your psaltries play,
    That good luck may
Come while the boy is a-teending.

   Drink now the strong beer,
    Cut the white loaf here,
The while the meat is a-shredding;
   For the rare mince-pie
    And the plums stand by
To fill the paste that's a-kneading.

                ROBERT HERRICK (1591–1674)

teending: kindling

CHRISTMAS

All after pleasures as I rid one day,
   My horse and I, both tir'd, body and mind,
   With full cry of affections, quite astray;
I took up in the next inn I could find.

There when I came, whom found I but my dear,
   My dearest Lord, expecting till the grief
   Of pleasures brought me to Him, ready there
To be all passengers' most sweet relief?

O Thou, whose glorious, yet contracted light,
   Wrapt in night's mantle, stole into a manger;
   Since my dark soul and brutish is Thy right,
To Man of all beasts be not Thou a stranger:

     Furnish and deck my soul, that thou mayst have
     A better lodging, than a rack, or grave.

The shepherds sing; and shall I silent be?
   My God, no hymn for thee?
My soul's a shepherd too: a flock it feeds
   Of thoughts, and words, and deeds.
The pasture is thy word; the streams, thy grace
   Enriching all the place.
Shepherd and flock shall sing, and all my powers
   Out-sing the daylight hours.
Then we will chide the sun for letting night
   Take up his place and right:

We sing one common Lord; wherefore he should
   Himself the candle hold.
I will go searching, till I find a sun
   Shall stay, till we have done;

A willing shiner that shall shine as gladly,
    As frost-nipped suns look sadly,
Then we will sing, and shine all our own day,
    And one another pay:
His beams shall cheer my breast, and both so twine,
Till ev'n his beams sing, and my music shine.

GEORGE HERBERT (1593–1633)

Journeys and places

THE SHEPHERD BOY'S CAROL

Can I not sing but hoy,
When the jolly shepherd made so much joy?

The shepherd upon a hill he sat;
He had on him his tabard and his hat,
His tarbox, his pipe, and his flagat;
His name was called Jolly, Jolly Wat,
 For he was a good herd boy,
  With hoy!
 For in his pipe he made so much joy.

The shepherd upon a hill was laid;
His dog to his girdle was tied;
He had not slept but a little spell
But 'Gloria in excelsis' was to him said.
  With hoy!
 For in his pipe he made so much joy.

The shepherd on a hill he stood;
Round about him his sheep they moved;
He put his hand under his hood;
He saw a star as red as blood.
  With hoy!
 For in his pipe he made so much joy.

'Now farewell Mall, and also Will;
For my love go ye all still

flagat: flageolet; *Mall, Will*: two of his sheep

Until I come again you till,
And evermore, Will, ring well thy bell.'
   With hoy!
   For in his pipe he made much joy.

'Now must I go where Christ is born;
Farewell, I come again tomorn;
Dog, keep well my sheep from the corn,
And warn well, warroke, when I blow my horn.'
   With hoy!
   For in his pipe he made much joy.

The shepherd said anon right,
'I will go to see yon fair sight,
Where the angel singeth on high,
And the star that shineth so bright.'
   With hoy!
   For in his pipe he made so much joy.

When Wat to Bedlem was come,
He sweat, he had gone so fast a pace.
He found Jesus in a simple place,
Between an ox and an ass.
   With hoy!
   For in his pipe he made so much joy.

'Jesus, I offer to thee here my pipe,
My skyrte, my tarbox and my scrype,
Home to my fellows now will I 'scape,
And also look unto my sheep.'
   With hoy!
   For in his pipe he made so much joy.

warroke: a puny child, here his helper; *Bedlem*: Bethlehem; *skyrte*: kilt; *scrype*: pouch

'Now, farewell, mine own herdsman, Wat.'
'Yea, for God, lady, even so I hat.
Lull well Jesus in thy lap,
And farewell, Joseph, with thy round cap.'
   With hoy!
   For in his pipe he made so much joy.

'Now may I well both hope and sing,
For I have been a Christ's bearing,
Home to my fellows now will I fling.
Christ of heaven to his bliss us bring!'
   With hoy!
   For in his pipe he made so much joy.

ANONYMOUS

hat: am called

JOURNEY OF THE MAGI

'A cold coming we had of it,
Just the worst time of the year
For a journey, and such a long journey:
The ways deep and the weather sharp,
The very dead of winter.'
And the camels galled, sore-footed, refractory,
Lying down in the melting snow.
There were times we regretted
The summer palaces on slopes, the terraces,
And the silken girls bringing sherbet.
Then the camel men cursing and grumbling
And running away, and wanting their liquor and women,

And the night-fires going out, and the lack of shelters,
And the cities hostile and the towns unfriendly
And the villages dirty and charging high prices:
A hard time we had of it.
At the end we preferred to travel all night,
Sleeping in snatches,
With the voices singing in our ears, saying
That this was all folly.

Then at dawn we came down to a temperate valley,
Wet, below the snow line, smelling of vegetation;
With a running stream and a water-mill beating the darkness,
And three trees on the low sky.
And an old white horse galloped away in the meadow.
Then we came to a tavern with vine-leaves over the lintel,
Six hands at an open door dicing for pieces of silver,
And feet kicking the empty wine-skins.
But there was no information, and so we continued
And arrived at evening, not a moment too soon
Finding the place; it was (you may say) satisfactory.

All this was a long time ago, I remember,
And I would do it again, but set down
This set down
This: were we led all that way for
Birth or Death? There was a Birth, certainly,
We had evidence and no doubt. I had seen birth and death,
But had thought they were different; this Birth was
Hard and bitter agony for us, like Death, our death.
We returned to our places, these Kingdoms,
But no longer at ease here, in the old dispensation,
With an alien people clutching their gods.
I shall be glad of another death.

T.S. ELIOT (1888–1965)

From RUNAGATE, RUNAGATE

Runs falls rises stumbles on from darkness into darkness
and the darkness thicketed with shapes of terror
and the hunters pursuing and the hounds pursuing
and the night cold and the night long and the river
to cross and the jack-muh-lanterns beckoning, beckoning
and blackness ahead and when shall I reach that somewhere
morning and keep on going and never turn back and keep on going

>   Runagate
>   Runagate
>   Runagate

Many thousands rise and go
many thousands crossing over
>   O mythic North
>   O star-shaped yonder Bible city

Some go weeping and some rejoicing
some in coffins and some in carriages
some in silks and some in shackles

> Rise and go or fare you well

No more auction block for me
no more driver's lash for me

> If you see my Pompey, 30 yrs of age,
> new breeches, plain stockings, negro shoes;
> If you see my Anna, likely young mulatto
> branded E on the right cheek, R on the left,
> catch them if you can and notify subscriber.

Catch them if you can, but it won't be easy.
They'll dart underground when you try to catch them,
plunge into quicksand, whirlpools, mazes,
turn into scorpions when you try to catch them

And before I'll be a slave
I'll be buried in my grave

    North star and bonanza gold
    I'm bound for the freedom, freedom-bound
    And oh Susyanna don't you cry for me

        Runagate
          Runagate
            Runagate

ROBERT HAYDEN (1913–80)

STANLEY MEETS MUTESA

Such a time of it they had;
The heat of the day
The chill of the night
And the mosquitoes that followed.
Such was the time and
They bound for a kingdom.

The thin weary line of carriers
With tattered dirty rags to cover their backs;
The battered bulky chests
That kept falling off their shaven heads.
Their tempers high and hot

The sun fierce and scorching
With it rose their spirits
With its fall their hopes
As each day sweated their bodies dry and
Flies clung in clumps on their sweat-scented backs.
Such was the march
And the hot season just breaking.

Each day a weary pony dropped
Left for the vultures on the plains;
Each afternoon a human skeleton collapsed,
Left for the Masai on the plains;
But the march trudged on
Its khaki leader in front
He the spirit that inspired.
He the light of hope.
Then came the afternoon of a hungry march,
A hot and hungry march it was;
The Nile and the Nyanza
Lay like two twins
Azure across the green countryside.
The march leapt on chaunting
Like young gazelles to a water hole.
Hearts beat faster
Loads felt lighter
As the cool water lapt their sore feet.
No more the dread of hungry hyenas
But only the tales of valour when
At Mutesa's court fires are lit.
No more the burning heat of the day
But song, laughter and dance.

The village looks on behind banana groves,
Children peer behind reed fences.
Such was the welcome.
No singing women to chaunt a welcome
Or drums to greet the white ambassador;
Only a few silent nods from aged faces
And one rumbling drum roll
To summon Mutesa's court to parley
For the country was not sure.

The gate of reeds is flung open,
There is silence
But only a moment's silence –
A silence of assessment.
The tall black king steps forward,
He towers over the thin bearded white man,
Then grabbing his lean white hand
Manages to whisper
'Mtu mweupe karibu'
White man you are welcome.
And the gate of polished reed closes behind them
And the West is let in.

JAMES D. RUBADIRI

THE ROAD NOT TAKEN

Two roads diverged in a yellow wood,
And sorry I could not travel both
And be one traveler, long I stood
And looked down one as far as I could
To where it bent in the undergrowth.

Then took the other, as just as fair,
And having perhaps the better claim,
Because it was grassy and wanted wear;
Though as far as that, the passing there
Had worn them really about the same.

And both that morning equally lay
In leaves no step had trodden black.
Oh, I kept the first for another day!
Yet knowing how way leads on to way,
I doubted if I should ever come back.

I shall be telling this with a sigh
Somewhere ages and ages hence:
Two roads diverged in a wood, and I –
I took the one less traveled by,
And that has made all the difference.

ROBERT FROST (1874–1963)

THE GREEN ROADS

The green roads that end in the forest
Are strewn with white goose feathers this June.

Like marks left behind by some one gone to the forest
To show his track. But he has never come back.

Down each green road a cottage looks at the forest.
Round one the nettle towers: two are bathed in flowers.

An old man along the green road to the forest
Strays from one, from another a child alone.

In the thicket bordering the forest,
All day long a thrush twiddles his song.

It is old, but the trees are young in the forest,
All but one like a castle keep, in the middle deep.

The oak saw the ages pass in the forest:
They were a host, but their memories are lost,

For the tree is dead: all things forget the forest
Excepting perhaps me, when now I see

The old man, the child, the goose feathers at the edge of the forest,
And hear all day long the thrush repeat his song.

EDWARD THOMAS (1878–1917)

From THE LADY OF SHALOTT

On either side the river lie
Long fields of barley and of rye,
That clothe the wold and meet the sky;
And thro' the field the road runs by
    To many-tower'd Camelot;
And up and down the people go,
Gazing where the lilies blow
Round an island there below,
    The island of Shalott.

Willows whiten, aspens quiver,
Little breezes dusk and shiver
Thro' the wave that runs for ever
By the island in the river
    Flowing down to Camelot.
Four gray walls, and four gray towers,
Overlook a space of flowers,
And the silent isle imbowers
    The Lady of Shalott.

By the margin, willow-veil'd,
Slide the heavy barges trail'd
By slow horses; and unhail'd
The shallop flitteth silken-sail'd
    Skimming down to Camelot:
But who hath seen her wave her hand?
Or at the casement seen her stand?
Or is she known in all the land,
    The Lady of Shalott?

Only reapers, reaping early
In among the bearded barley,
Hear a song that echoes cheerly
From the river winding clearly,
   Down to tower'd Camelot:
And by the moon the reaper weary,
Piling sheaves in uplands airy,
Listening, whispers, ''Tis the fairy
   Lady of Shalott.'

               ALFRED,
               LORD TENNYSON (1809–92)

THE WAY THROUGH THE WOODS

They shut the road through the woods
   Seventy years ago.
Weather and rain have undone it again,
   And now you would never know
There was once a road through the woods
   Before they planted the trees.
It is under the coppice and heath,
   And the thin anemones.
   Only the keeper sees
That, where the ring-dove broods,
   And the badgers roll at ease,
There was once a road through the woods.

Yet, if you enter the woods
   Of a summer evening late,
When the night-air cools on the trout-ringed pools
   Where the otter whistles his mate,

(They fear not men in the woods
    Because they see so few),
You will hear the beat of a horse's feet
    And the swish of a skirt in the dew,
    Steadily cantering through
The misty solitudes
    As though they perfectly knew
The old lost road through the woods . . .
But there is no road through the woods!

RUDYARD KIPLING
(1865–1936)

THE ROLLING ENGLISH ROAD

Before the Roman came to Rye or out to Severn strode,
The rolling English drunkard made the rolling English road.
A reeling road, a rolling road, that rambles round the shire,
And after him the parson ran, the sexton and the squire;
A merry road, a mazy road, and such as we did tread
The night we went to Birmingham by way of Beachy Head.

I knew no harm of Bonaparte and plenty of the Squire,
And for to fight the Frenchman I did not much desire;
But I did bash their baggonets because they came array'd
To straighten out the crooked road an English drunkard made,
Where you and I went down the lane with ale-mugs in our hands,
The night we went to Glastonbury by way of Goodwin Sands.

His sins they were forgiven him; or why do flowers run
Behind him; and the hedges all strengthening in the sun?
The wild thing went from left to right and knew not which was which,
But the wild rose was above him when they found him in the ditch.
God pardon us, nor harden us; we did not see so clear
The night we went to Bannockburn by way of Brighton Pier.

My friends, we will not go again or ape an ancient rage,
Or stretch the folly of our youth to be the shame of age,
But walk with clearer eyes and ears this path that wandereth,
And see undrugg'd in evening light the decent inn of death;
For there is good news yet to hear and fine things to be seen
Before we go to Paradise by way of Kensal Green.

G. K. CHESTERTON
(1874–1936)

THE OLD SHIPS

I have seen old ships sail like swans asleep
Beyond the village which men still call Tyre,
With leaden age o'ercargoed, dipping deep
For Famagusta and the hidden sun
That rings black Cyprus with a lake of fire;
And all those ships were certainly so old,
Who knows how oft with squat and noisy gun,
Questing brown slaves or Syrian oranges,
The pirate Genoese
Hell-raked them till they rolled
Blood, water, fruit and corpses up the hold.
But now through friendly seas they softly run,
Painted the mid-sea blue or shore-sea green,
Still patterned with the vine and grapes in gold.

But I have seen,
Pointing her shapely shadows from the dawn
An image tumbled on a rose-swept bay,
A drowsy ship of some yet older day;
And, wonder's breath indrawn,
Thought I – who knows – who knows – but in that same
(Fished up beyond Aeaea, patched up new
– Stern painted brighter blue –)
That talkative, bald-headed seaman came
(Twelve patient comrades sweating at the oar)
From Troy's doom-crimson shore,
And with great lies about his wooden horse
Set the crew laughing, and forgot his course.

It was so old a ship – who knows, who knows?
And yet so beautiful, I watched in vain
To see the mast burst open with a rose,
And the whole deck put on its leaves again.

JAMES ELROY FLECKER
(1884–1915)

I LIKE TO SEE IT LAP THE MILES

I like to see it lap the Miles –
And lick the Valleys up –
And stop to feed itself at Tanks –
And then – prodigious step

Around a Pile of Mountains –
And supercilious peer
In Shanties – by the sides of Roads –
And then a Quarry pare

To fit its Ribs
And crawl between
Complaining all the while
In horrid hooting stanza –
Then chase itself down Hill –

And neigh like Boanerges –
Then – punctual as a Star
Stop – docile and omnipotent
At its own stable door.

EMILY DICKINSON (1830–86)

NIGHT MAIL
(Commentary for a Post Office film)

I

This is the Night Mail crossing the Border,
Bringing the cheque and the postal order.

Letters for the rich, letters for the poor,
The shop at the corner, the girl next door.

Pulling up Beattock, a steady climb:
The gradient's against her, but she's on time.

Past cotton-grass and moorland border,
Shovelling white steam over her shoulder.

Snorting noisily, she passes
Silent miles of wind-bent grasses.

Birds turn their heads as she approaches,
Stare from bushes at her blank-faced coaches.

Sheep-dogs cannot turn her course;
They slumber on with paws across.

In the farm she passes no one wakes,
But a jug in a bedroom gently shakes.

II
Dawn freshens. Her climb is done.
Down towards Glasgow she descends,
Towards the steam tugs yelping down a glade of cranes,
Towards the fields of apparatus, the furnaces
Set on the dark plain like gigantic chessmen.
All Scotland waits for her:
In dark glens, beside pale-green lochs,
Men long for news.

III
Letters of thanks, letters from banks,
Letters of joy from girl and boy,
Receipted bills and invitations
To inspect new stock or to visit relations,
And applications for situations,
And timid lovers' declarations.
And gossip, gossip from the nations.
News circumstantial, news financial,
Letters with holiday snaps to enlarge in,
Letters with faces scrawled in the margin,
Letters from uncles, cousins and aunts,
Letters to Scotland from the South of France,
Letters of condolence to Highlands and Lowlands,

Written on paper of every hue,
The pink, the violet, the white and the blue,
The chatty, the catty, the boring, the adoring,
The cold and official and the heart's outpouring,
Clever, stupid, short and long,
The typed and the printed and the spelt all wrong.

IV

Thousands are still asleep,
Dreaming of terrifying monsters
Or a friendly tea beside the band in Cranston's or Crawford's:
Asleep in working Glasgow, asleep in well-set Edinburgh,
Asleep in granite Aberdeen,
They continue their dreams,
But shall wake soon and hope for letters,
And none will hear the postman's knock
Without a quickening of the heart,
For who can bear to feel himself forgotten?

W.H. AUDEN (1907–73)

ADLESTROP

Yes, I remember Adlestrop –
The name, because one afternoon
Of heat the express-train drew up there
Unwontedly. It was late June.

The steam hissed. Someone cleared his throat.
No one left and no one came
On the bare platform. What I saw
Was Adlestrop – only the name

And willows, willow-herb, and grass,
And meadowsweet, and haycocks dry,
No whit less still and lonely fair
Than the high cloudlets in the sky.

And for that minute a blackbird sang
Close by, and round him, mistier,
Farther and farther, all the birds
Of Oxfordshire and Gloucestershire.

EDWARD THOMAS (1878–1917)

TRAVELLING HOME

The train. A hot July. On either hand
Our sober, fruitful, unemphatic land,
This Cambridge country, plain beneath the sky
Where I was born, and grew, and hope to die.

Look! where the willows hide a rushy pool,
And the old horse goes squelching down to cool,
One angler's rod against their silvery green,
Still seen today as once by Bewick seen.

A cottage there, thatched sadly, like its earth,
Where crimson ramblers make a short-lived mirth;
Here, only flies the flick-tail cows disturb
Among the shaven meads and willow-herb.

Bewick: Thomas Bewick, 1753–1828, wood engraver

There, rounded hay-ricks solemn in the yard,
Barns gravely, puritanically tarred,
Next heavy elms that guard the ripening grain
And fields, and elms, and corn, and fields again.

Over the soft savannahs of the corn,
Like ships the hot white butterflies are borne,
While clouds pass slowly on the flower-blue dome
Like spirits in a vast and peaceful home.

Over the dyke I watch their shadows flow
As the Icenian watched them long ago;
So let me in this Cambridge calm July
Fruitfully live and undistinguished die.

FRANCES CORNFORD
(1886–1960)

Icenian: ancient British tribe

AMERICAN NAMES

I have fallen in love with American names,
The sharp names that never get fat,
The makeshift titles of mining-claims,
The plumed war-bonnet of Medicine Hat,
Tucson and Deadwood and Lost Mule Flat.

Seine and Piave are silver spoons,
But the spoonbowl-metal is thin and worn,
There are English counties like hunting-tunes
Played on the keys of a postboy's horn,
But I will remember where I was born.

I will remember Carquinez Straits,
Little French Lick and Lundy's Lane,
The Yankee ships and the Yankee dates
And the bullet-towns of Calamity Jane.
I will remember Skunktown Plain.

I will fall in love with a Salem tree
And a rawhide quirt from Santa Cruz,
I will get me a bottle of Boston sea
And a blue-gum nigger to sing me blues.
I am tired of loving a foreign muse.

Rue des Martyrs and Bleeding-Heart-Yard,
Senlis, Pisa, and Blindman's Oast,
It is a magic ghost you guard
But I am sick for a newer ghost,
Harrisburg, Spartanburg, Painted Post.

Henry and John were never so
And Henry and John were always right?
Granted, but when it was time to go
And the tea and the laurels had stood all night
Did they never watch for Nantucket Light?

quirt: whip

I shall not rest quiet in Montparnasse.
I shall not lie easy at Winchelsea.
You may bury my body in Sussex grass,
You may bury my tongue at Champmédy,
I shall not be there. I shall rise and pass.
Bury my heart at Wounded Knee.

STEPHEN VINCENT BENET
(1898–1943)

IN THE HIGHLANDS

In the highlands, in the country places,
Where the old plain men have rosy faces,
   And the young fair maidens
     Quiet eyes;
Where essential silence cheers and blesses,
And for ever in the hill-recesses
   Her more lovely music
     Broods and dies –

O to mount again where erst I haunted;
Where the old red hills are bird-enchanted,
   And the low green meadows
     Bright with sward;
And when even dies, the million-tinted,
And the night has come, and planets glinted,
   Lo, the valley hollow
     Lamp-bestarr'd!

O to dream, O to awake and wander
There, and with delight to take and render,
   Through the trance of silence,
     Quiet breath!
Lo! for there, among the flowers and grasses,
Only the mightier movement sounds and passes;
   Only winds and rivers,
     Life and death.

ROBERT LOUIS
STEVENSON (1850–94)

THE MAP

Land lies in water; it is shadowed green.
Shadows, or are they shallows, at its edges
showing the line of long sea-weeded ledges
where weeds hang to the simple blue from green.
Or does the land lean down to lift the sea from under,
drawing it unperturbed around itself?
Along the fine tan sandy shelf
is the land tugging at the sea from under?

The shadow of Newfoundland lies flat and still.
Labrador's yellow, where the moony Eskimo
has oiled it. We can stroke these lovely bays,
under a glass as if they were expected to blossom,
or as if to provide a clean cage for invisible fish.
The names of seashore towns run out to sea,
the names of cities cross the neighboring mountains
– the printer here experiencing the same excitement
as when emotion too far exceeds its cause.

These peninsulas take the water between thumb and finger
like women feeling for the smoothness of yard-goods.

Mapped waters are more quiet than the land is,
lending the land their waves' own conformation:
and Norway's hare runs south in agitation,
profiles investigate the sea, where land is.
Are they assigned, or can the countries pick their colors?
– What suits the character or the native workers best.
Topography displays no favorites; North's as West.
More delicate than the historians are the map-makers' colors.

ELIZABETH BISHOP (1911–79)

IF I SHOULD EVER BY CHANCE

If I should ever by chance grow rich
I'll buy Codham, Cockridden, and Childerditch,
Roses, Pyrgo, and Lapwater,
And let them all to my elder daughter.
The rent I shall ask of her will be only
Each year's first violets, white and lonely,
The first primroses and orchises –
She must find them before I do, that is.
But if she finds a blossom on furze
Without rent they shall all for ever be hers,
Whenever I am sufficiently rich:
Codham, Cockridden, and Childerditch,
Roses, Pyrgo and Lapwater –
I shall give them all to my elder daughter.

EDWARD THOMAS (1878–1917)

WHAT SHALL I GIVE?

What shall I give my daughter the younger
More than will keep her from cold and hunger?
I shall not give her anything.
If she shared South Weald and Havering,
Their acres, the two brooks running between,
Paine's Brook and Weald Brook,
With peewit, woodpecker, swan, and rook,
She would be no richer than the queen
Who once on a time sat in Havering Bower
Alone, with the shadows, pleasure and power.
She could do no more with Samarcand,
Or the mountains of a mountain land
And its far white house above cottages
Like Venus above the Pleiades.
Her small hands I would not cumber
With so many acres and their lumber,
But leave her Steep and her own world
And her spectacled self with hair uncurled,
Wanting a thousand little things
That time without contentment brings.

EDWARD THOMAS (1878–1917)

BINSEY POPLARS
FELLED 1879

My aspens dear, whose airy cages quelled,
Quelled or quenched in leaves the leaping sun,
All felled, felled, are all felled;
   Of a fresh and following folded rank
      Not spared, not one
      That dandled a sandalled
   Shadow that swam or sank
On meadow and river and wind-wandering
                   weed-winding bank.

O if we but knew what we do
     When we delve or hew –
   Hack and rack the growing green!
     Since country is so tender
   To touch, her being so slender,
   That, like this sleek and seeing ball
   But a prick will make no eye at all,
     Where we, even where we mean
        To mend her we end her,
       When we hew or delve:
After-comers cannot guess the beauty been.
   Ten or twelve, only ten or twelve
     Strokes of havoc unselve
       The sweet especial scene,
     Rural scene, a rural scene,
     Sweet especial rural scene.

GERARD MANLEY HOPKINS
(1844–89)

COMPOSED UPON WESTMINSTER BRIDGE

Earth has not anything to show more fair:
Dull would he be of soul who could pass by
A sight so touching in its majesty:
This City now doth, like a garment, wear
The beauty of the morning; silent, bare,
Ships, towers, domes, theatres, and temples lie
Open unto the fields, and to the sky;
All bright and glittering in the smokeless air.
Never did sun more beautifully steep
In his first splendour, valley, rock, or hill;
Ne'er saw I, never felt, a calm so deep!
The river glideth at his own sweet will:
Dear God! the very houses seem asleep;
And all that mighty heart is lying still!

WILLIAM WORDSWORTH
(1770–1850)

LANDSCAPES

I. New Hampshire

Children's voices in the orchard
Between the blossom- and the fruit-time:
Golden head, crimson head,
Between the green tip and the root.
Black wing, brown wing, hover over;
Twenty years and the spring is over;
To-day grieves, to-morrow grieves,
Cover me over, light-in-leaves;

Golden head, black wing,
Cling, swing,
Spring, sing,
Swing up into the apple-tree.

II. Virginia

Red river, red river,
Slow flow heat is silence
No will is still as a river
Still. Will heat move
Only through the mocking-bird
Heard once? Still hills
Wait. Gates wait. Purple trees,
White trees, wait, wait,
Delay, decay. Living, living,
Never moving. Ever moving
Iron thoughts came with me
And go with me:
Red river, river, river.

III. Usk

Do not suddenly break the branch, or
Hope to find
The white hart behind the white well.
Glance aside, not for lance, do not spell
Old enchantments. Let them sleep.
'Gently dip, but not too deep',
Lift your eyes
Where the roads dip and where the roads rise
Seek only there
Where the grey light meets the green air
The hermit's chapel, the pilgrim's prayer.

IV. Rannoch, by Glencoe

Here the crow starves, here the patient stag
Breeds for the rifle. Between the soft moor
And the soft sky, scarcely room
To leap or soar. Substance crumbles, in the thin air
Moon cold or moon hot. The road winds in
Listlessness of ancient war,
Languor of broken steel,
Clamour of confused wrong, apt
In silence. Memory is strong
Beyond the bone. Pride snapped,
Shadow of pride is long, in the long pass
No concurrence of bone.

V. Cape Ann

O quick quick quick, quick hear the song-sparrow,
Swamp-sparrow, fox-sparrow, vesper-sparrow
At dawn and dusk. Follow the dance
Of the goldfinch at noon. Leave to chance
The Blackburnian warbler, the shy one. Hail
With shrill whistle the note of the quail, the bob-white
Dodging by bay-bush. Follow the feet
Of the walker, the water-thrush. Follow the flight
Of the dancing arrow, the purple martin. Greet
In silence the bullbat. All are delectable. Sweet sweet sweet
But resign this land at the end, resign it
To its true owner, the tough one, the sea-gull.

The palaver is finished.

T.S. ELIOT (1888–1965)

Spells, magic and mystery

SPELLS

I dance and dance without any feet –
This is the spell of the ripening wheat.

With never a tongue I've a tale to tell –
This is the meadow-grasses' spell.

I give you health without any fee –
This is the spell of the apple-tree.

I rhyme and riddle without any book –
This is the spell of the bubbling brook.

Without any legs I run for ever –
This is the spell of the mighty river.

I fall for ever and not at all –
This is the spell of the waterfall.

Without a voice I roar aloud –
This is the spell of the thunder-cloud.

No button or seam has my white coat –
This is the spell of the leaping goat.

I can cheat strangers with never a word –
This is the spell of the cuckoo-bird.

We have tongues in plenty but speak no names –
This is the spell of the fiery flames.

The creaking door has a spell to riddle –
I play a tune without any fiddle.

JAMES REEVES (1909–78)

I HAVE FOUR SISTERS BEYOND THE SEA

I have four sisters beyond the sea,
    Perrie, Merrie, Dixie, Dominie;
And they each sent a present unto me,
    Petrum, Partrum, Paradisi, Temporie,
    Perrie, Merrie, Dixie, Dominie.

The first sent a chicken, without e'er a bone,
    Perrie, Merrie, Dixie, Dominie;
The second a cherry, without e'er a stone,
    Petrum, Partrum, Paradisi, Temporie,
    Perrie, Merrie, Dixie, Dominie.

The third sent a book which no man could read,
    Perrie, Merrie, Dixie, Dominie;
The fourth sent a blanket, without e'er a thread,
    Petrum, Partrum, Paradisi, Temporie,
    Perrie, Merrie, Dixie, Dominie.

How can there be a chicken without e'er a bone?
    Perrie, Merrie, Dixie, Dominie;
How can there be a cherry without e'er a stone?
    Petrum, Partrum, Paradisi, Temporie,
    Perrie, Merrie, Dixie, Dominie.

How can there be a book which no man can read?
    Perrie, Merrie, Dixie, Dominie;
How can there be a blanket without e'er a thread?
    Petrum, Partrum, Paradisi, Temporie,
    Perrie, Merrie, Dixie, Dominie.

When the chicken's in the egg-shell there is no bone,
   Perrie, Merrie, Dixie, Dominie;
When the cherry's in the bud, there is no stone,
   Petrum, Partrum, Paradisi, Temporie,
   Perrie, Merrie, Dixie, Dominie.

When the book's in the press, no man it can read,
   Perrie, Merrie, Dixie, Dominie;
When the blanket's in the fleece there is no thread,
   Petrum, Partrum, Paradisi, Temporie,
   Perrie, Merrie, Dixie, Dominie.

ANONYMOUS

ARIEL'S SONGS

Come unto these yellow sands,
   And then take hands:
Curtsied when you have, and kiss'd, –
   The wild waves whist, –
Foot it featly here and there;
And, sweet sprites, the burden bear,
   Hark, hark!
   Bow, wow,
   The watch-dogs bark:
   Bow, wow,
   Hark, hark! I hear
The strain of strutting Chanticleer
   Cry, cock-a-diddle-dow.

The Tempest, I ii

Full fathom five thy father lies;
   Of his bones are coral made;
Those are pearls that were his eyes:
   Nothing of him that doth fade,
But doth suffer a sea-change
Into something rich and strange.
Sea-nymphs hourly ring his knell.
Hark! now I hear them, – Ding-dong, bell.

The Tempest, I ii

Where the bee sucks, there suck I:
In a cowslip's bell I lie;
There I couch when owls do cry.
On the bat's back I do fly
After summer merrily.
Merrily, merrily shall I live now
Under the blossom that hangs on the bough.

The Tempest, V i

FAIRY SONG

Over hill, over dale,
   Thorough bush, thorough brier,
Over park, over pale,
   Thorough flood, thorough fire.
I do wander everywhere,
Swifter than the moon's sphere;
And I serve the fairy queen,
To dew her orbs upon the green.

The cowslips tall her pensioners be;
In their gold coats spots you see;
Those be rubies, fairy favours,
In those freckles live their savours.

A Midsummer Night's Dream, II i

THE FAIRIES SING TITANIA TO SLEEP

You spotted snakes with double tongue,
   Thorny hedgehogs, be not seen;
Newts and blind-worms, do no wrong,
   Come not near our fairy queen.

   Philomel, with melody,
   Sing in our sweet lullaby.
Lulla, lulla, lullaby, lulla, lulla, lullaby:
     Never harm,
     Nor spell, nor charm:
     Come our lovely lady nigh;
     So, good night, with lullaby.

Weaving spiders, come not here;
   Hence, you long-legg'd spinners, hence!
Beetles black, approach not near;
   Worm nor snail, do no offence.

A Midsummer Night's Dream, II ii

PUCK'S EPILOGUE

Now the hungry lion roars
   And the wolf behowls the moon;
Whilst the heavy ploughman snores.
   All with weary task foredone.
Now the wasted brands do glow,
   Whilst the screech-owl, screeching loud,
Puts the wretch that lies in woe
   In remembrance of a shroud.
Now it is the time of night
   That the graves, all gaping wide,
Every one lets forth his sprite,
   In the church-way paths to glide;
And we fairies, that do run
   By the triple Hecate's team,
From the presence of the sun,
   Following darkness like a dream,
Now are frolic; not a mouse
Shall disturb this hallow'd house:
I am sent with broom before,
To sweep the dust behind the door.

                    WILLIAM SHAKESPEARE
                    (1564–1616)
                    A Midsummer Night's Dream, V i

SONG

Go and catch a falling star,
   Get with child a mandrake root,
Tell me where all past years are,
   Or who cleft the Devil's foot;
Teach me to hear mermaids singing,
Or to keep off envy's stinging,
      And find
      What wind
Serves to advance an honest mind.

If thou be'st born to strange sights,
   Things invisible to see,
Ride ten thousand days and nights
   Till Age snow white hairs on thee;
Thou, when thou return'st, wilt tell me
All strange wonders that befell thee,
      And swear
      No where
Lives a woman true and fair.

If thou find'st one, let me know;
   Such a pilgrimage were sweet.
Yet do not; I would not go,
   Though at next door we might meet.
Though she were true when you met her,
And last till you write your letter.
      Yet she
      Will be
False, ere I come, to two or three.

JOHN DONNE (1572?–1631)

LUCY ASHTON'S SONG

Look not thou on beauty's charming,
Sit thou still when kings are arming,
Taste not when the wine-cup glistens,
Speak not when the people listens,
Stop thy ear against the singer,
From the red gold keep thy finger;
Vacant heart and hand and eye,
Easy live and quiet die.

SIR WALTER SCOTT
(1771–1832)
From *The Bride of Lammermoor*

KUBLA KHAN

In Xanadu did Kubla Khan
A stately pleasure-dome decree:
Where Alph, the sacred river, ran
Through caverns measureless to man
    Down to a sunless sea.
So twice five miles of fertile ground
With walls and towers were girdled round:
And here were gardens bright with sinuous rills,
Where blossom'd many an incense-bearing tree;
And here were forests ancient as the hills,
Enfolding sunny spots of greenery.

But O, that deep romantic chasm which slanted
Down the green hill athwart a cedarn cover!
A savage place! as holy and enchanted
As e'er beneath a waning moon was haunted

By woman wailing for her demon-lover!
And from this chasm, with ceaseless turmoil seething,
As if this earth in fast thick pants were breathing,
A mighty fountain momently was forced;
Amid whose swift half-intermittent burst
Huge fragments vaulted like rebounding hail,
Or chaffy grain beneath the thresher's flail:
And 'mid these dancing rocks at once and ever
It flung up momently the sacred river.
Five miles meandering with a mazy motion
Through wood and dale the sacred river ran,
Then reach'd the caverns measureless to man,
And sank in tumult to a lifeless ocean:
And 'mid this tumult Kubla heard from far
Ancestral voices prophesying war!

The shadow of the dome of pleasure
   Floated midway on the waves;
Where was heard the mingled measure
   From the fountain and the caves.
It was a miracle of rare device,
A sunny pleasure-dome with caves of ice!

   A damsel with a dulcimer
      In a vision once I saw:
   It was an Abyssinian maid,
      And on her dulcimer she play'd,
   Singing of Mount Abora.
   Could I revive within me,
     Her symphony and song,
To such a deep delight 'twould win me,
That with music loud and long,
I would build that dome in air,
That sunny dome! those caves of ice!

And all who heard should see them there,
And all should cry, Beware! Beware!
   His flashing eyes, his floating hair!
  Weave a circle round him thrice,
    And close your eyes with holy dread,
    For he on honey-dew hath fed,
  And drunk the milk of Paradise.

                        SAMUEL TAYLOR
                        COLERIDGE (1772–1834)

SONG OF THE MAD PRINCE

  Who said, 'Peacock Pie'?
    The old King to the sparrow:
  Who said, 'Crops are ripe'?
    Rust to the harrow:
  Who said, 'Where sleeps she now?
    Where rests she now her head,
  Bathed in eve's loveliness'? –
    That's what I said.

  Who said, 'Ay, mum's the word'?;
    Sexton to willow:
  Who said, 'Green dusk for dreams.
    Moss for a pillow'?
  Who said, 'All Time's delight
    Hath she for narrow bed;
  Life's troubled bubble broken'? –
    That's what I said.

                        WALTER DE LA MARE
                        (1873–1956)

WITCHES' SONG

Thrice the brinded cat hath mew'd.
Thrice, and once the hedge-pig whin'd.
Harpier cries: ''Tis time, 'tis time.'
Round about the cauldron go;
In the poison'd entrails throw.
Toad, that under cold stone
Days and nights has thirty-one
Swelter'd venom sleeping got,
Boil thou first i' the charmed pot.
    Double, double toil and trouble;
    Fire burn and cauldron bubble.
Fillet of a fenny snake,
In the cauldron boil and bake;
Eye of newt, and toe of frog,
Wool of bat, and tongue of dog,
Adder's fork, and blind-worm's sting,
Lizard's leg, and howlet's wing,
For a charm of powerful trouble,
Like a hell-broth boil and bubble.
    Double, double toil and trouble;
    Fire burn and cauldron bubble.

Scale of dragon, tooth of wolf,
Witches' mummy, maw and gulf
Of the ravin'd salt-sea shark,
Root of hemlock digg'd i' the dark,
Liver of blaspheming Jew,
Gall of goat, and slips of yew
Sliver'd in the moon's eclipse,
Nose of Turk and Tartar's lips,
Finger of birth-strangled babe

Ditch-deliver'd by a drab,
Make the gruel thick and slab:
Add thereto a tiger's chaudron,
For the ingredients of our cauldron.
   Double, double toil and trouble;
   Fire burn and cauldron bubble,
   Cool it with a baboon's blood,
   Then the charm is firm and good.

WILLIAM SHAKESPEARE
(1564–1616)
Macbeth, IV i

THE WITCHES' CHARMS

Charm I

Dame, dame! the watch is set:
Quickly come, we all are met.
From the lakes and from the fens,
From the rocks and from the dens,
From the woods and from the caves,
From the churchyards, from the graves,
From the dungeon, from the tree
That they die on, here are we!
   Comes she not yet?
   Strike another heat!

Charm II

The weather is fair, the wind is good:
Up, dame, o' your horse of wood!
Or else tuck up your gray frock,
And saddle your goat or your green cock,

And make his bridle a bottom of thrid
To roll up how many miles you have rid.
Quickly come away,
For we all stay.
  Not yet? nay then
  We'll try her again.

          Charm III
The owl is abroad, the bat and the toad,
  And so is the cat-a-mountain;
The ant and the mole sit both in a hole,
And frog peeps out o' the fountain.
  The dogs they do bay, and the timbrels play,
    The spindle is now a-turning;
The moon it is red, and the stars are fled,
  But all the sky is a-burning:
The ditch is made, and our nails the spade:
With pictures full, of wax and of wool;
Their livers I stick with needles quick;
There lacks but the blood to make up the flood.
  Quickly, dame, then bring your part in!
  Spur, spur upon little Martin!
  Merrily, merrily, make him sail,
  A worm in his mouth, and a thorn in 's tail,
  Fire above, and fire below,
  With a whip i' your hand to make him go!
O, now, she's come!
Let all be dumb.

                        BEN JONSON (1572/3–1637)
                            The Masque of Queens

bottom of thrid: ball of thread; *cat-a-mountain*: wild cat;
Martin: the spirit in the shape of a goat who summons the witches

WINDY NIGHTS

Whenever the moon and stars are set,
   Whenever the wind is high,
All night long in the dark and wet,
   A man goes riding by.
Late in the night when the fires are out,
Why does he gallop and gallop about?

Whenever the trees are crying aloud,
   And ships are tossed at sea,
By, on the highway, low and loud,
   By at the gallop goes he.
By at the gallop he goes, and then
By he comes back at the gallop again.

ROBERT LOUIS
STEVENSON (1850–94)

From GOBLIN MARKET

Morning and evening
Maids heard the goblins cry:
'Come buy our orchard fruits,
Come buy, come buy:
Apples and quinces,
Lemons and oranges,
Plump unpecked cherries,
Melons and raspberries,
Bloom-down-cheeked peaches,
Swart-headed mulberries,
Wild free-born cranberries,

Crab-apples, dewberries,
Pineapples, blackberries,
Apricots, strawberries;
All ripe together
In summer weather —
Morns that pass by,
Fair eves that fly;
Come buy, come buy:
Our grapes fresh from the vine,
Pomegranates full and fine,
Dates and sharp bullaces,
Rare pears and greengages,
Damsons and bilberries,
Taste them and try;
Currants and gooseberries,
Bright-fire-like barberries,
Figs to fill your mouth,
Citrons from the South,
Sweet to tongue and sound to eye;
Come buy, come buy.'

   Evening by evening
Among the brookside rushes,
Laura bowed her head to hear,
Lizzie veiled her blushes:
Crouching close together
In the cooling weather,
With clasping arms and cautioning lips,
With tingling cheeks and finger tips.
'Lie close,' Laura said,
Pricking up her golden head:
'We must not look at goblin men,

We must not buy their fruits:
Who knows upon what soil they fed
Their hungry thirsty roots?'
'Come buy,' call the goblins
Hobbling down the glen.
'Oh,' cried Lizzie, 'Laura, Laura,
You should not peep at goblin men.'
Lizzie covered up her eyes,
Covered close lest they should look;
Laura raised her glossy head,
And whispered like the restless brook:
'Look, Lizzie, look, Lizzie,
Down the glen tramp little men.
One hauls a basket,
One bears a plate,
One lugs a golden dish
Of many pounds weight.
How fair the vine must grow
Whose grapes are so luscious;
How warm the wind must blow
Through those fruit bushes.'
'No,' said Lizzie: 'No, no, no;
Their offers should not charm us,
Their evil gifts would harm us.'
She thrust a dimpled finger
In each ear, shut eyes and ran:
Curious Laura chose to linger
Wondering at each merchant man.
One had a cat's face,
One whisked a tail,
One tramped at a rat's pace,
One crawled like a snail,

One like a wombat prowled obtuse and furry,
One like a ratel tumbled hurry-skurry.
She heard a voice like voice of doves
Cooing all together:
They sounded kind and full of loves
In the pleasant weather.
. . . . . .
   Backwards up the mossy glen
Turned and trooped the goblin men,
With their shrill repeated cry,
'Come buy, come buy.'

CHRISTINA ROSSETTI
(1830–94)

THE STOLEN CHILD

Where dips the rocky highland
Of Sleuth Wood in the lake,
There lies a leafy island
Where flapping herons wake
The drowsy water-rats;
There we've hid our faery vats,
Full of berries
And of reddest stolen cherries.
Come away, O human child!
To the waters and the wild
With a faery, hand in hand,
For the world's more full of weeping than you can understand.

Where the wave of moonlight glosses
The dim grey sands with light,
Far off by furthest Rosses
We foot it all the night,
Weaving olden dances,
Mingling hands and mingling glances
Till the moon has taken flight;
To and fro we leap
And chase the froth bubbles,
While the world is full of troubles
And is anxious in its sleep.
Come away, O human child!
To the waters and the wild
With a faery, hand in hand,
For the world's more full of weeping than you can understand.

Where the wandering water gushes
From the hills above Glen-Car,
In pools among the rushes
That scarce could bathe a star,
We seek for slumbering trout
And whispering in their ears
Give them unquiet dreams;
Leaning softly out
From ferns that drop their tears
Over the young streams.
Come away, O human child!
To the waters and the wild
With a faery, hand in hand,
For the world's more full of weeping than you can understand.

Away with us he's going,
The solemn-eyed:
He'll hear no more the lowing
Of the calves on the warm hillside
Or the kettle on the hob
Sing peace into his breast,
Or see the brown mice bob
Round and round the oatmeal-chest.
For he comes, the human child,
To the waters and the wild
With a faery, hand in hand,
From a world more full of weeping than he can understand.

W.B. YEATS (1865–1939)

TWO CORPUS CHRISTI CAROLS

Lully, lulley, lully, lulley,
The falcon hath borne my mate away.

He bore him up, he bore him down;
He bore him into an orchard brown.
   Lully, lulley, lully, lulley,
   The falcon hath borne my mate away.

In that orchard there was an hall,
That was hangèd with purple and pall.
   Lully, lulley, lully, lulley,
   The falcon hath borne my mate away.

And in that hall there was a bed,
That was hangèd with gold so red.
   Lully, lulley, lully, lulley,
   The falcon hath borne my mate away.

And on that bed there lieth a knight,
His woundes bleeding day and night.
   Lully, lulley, lully, lulley,
   The falcon hath borne my mate away.

By that bed side there kneeleth a maid,
And she weepeth both night and day.
   Lully, lulley, lully, lulley,
   The falcon hath borne my mate away.

By that bed side there standeth a stone,
Corpus Christi written thereon.
   Lully, lulley, lully, lulley,
   The falcon has stolen my mate away.

ANONYMOUS

   pall: rich fabric

The heron flew east, the heron flew west,
The heron flew to the fair forest;
She flew o'er streams and meadows green,
And a' to see what could be seen:
And when she saw the faithful pair,
Her breast grew sick, her head grew sair;
For there she saw a lovely bower,
Was a' clad o'er wi' lilly-flower;
And in that bower there was a bed
With silken sheets, and weel down spread:
And in the bed there lay a knight,
Whose wounds did bleed both day and night;

And by the bed there stood a stane,
And there was set a leal maiden,
With silver needle and silken thread,
Stemming the wounds when they did bleed.

ANONYMOUS

leal: loyal

THOU GREAT GOD

Thou great God that dwellest in Heaven,
Thou art the shield, the stronghold of truth.
'Tis Thou, and Thou alone, that dwellest in the highest,
Thou the maker of life and the skies,
Thou the maker of the sparse and clustered stars,
As the shooting-star doth proclaim.
The horn soundeth aloud, calling us
To thee, great Hunter, Hunter of souls,
Who maketh one herd of friend and foe,
All covered and sheltered under Thy cloak.
Thou art the little Lamb, Mesiyas,
Whose hands are wounded with nailing,
Thy blood that streameth for ever and ever
For the sake of us men was shed.

ANONYMOUS

From the Xhosa, trans. A.C. Jordan

Strange tales

THERE WAS A LADY ALL SKIN AND BONE

There was a lady all skin and bone,
Sure such a lady was never known:
It happened upon a certain day,
This lady went to church to pray.

When she came to the church stile,
There she did rest a little while;
When she came to the church yard,
There the bells so loud she heard.

When she came to the church door,
She stopped to rest a little more;
When she came to the church within,
The parson prayed 'gainst pride and sin.

On looking up, on looking down,
She saw a dead man on the ground;
And from his nose unto his chin,
The worms crawled out, the worms crawled in.

Then she unto the parson said,
Shall I be so when I am dead?
O yes! O yes, the parson said,
You will be so when you are dead.

ANONYMOUS

THE WIFE OF USHER'S WELL

There lived a wife at Usher's Well
   And a wealthy wife was she;
She had three stout and stalwart sons
   And sent them o'er the sea.

They hadna been a week from her,
   A week but barely one,
When word came to the carline wife
   That her three sons were gone.

They hadna been a week from her,
   A week but barely three,
When word came to the carline wife
   That her sons she'd never see.

'I wish the wind may never cease,
   Nor fishes in the flood,
Till my three sons come home to me
   In earthly flesh and blood.'

It fell about the Martinmas
   When nights are lang and mirk,
The carline wife's three sons came home,
   And their hats were of the birk.

It neither grew in stream nor ditch,
   Nor yet in any sheugh,
But at the gate of Paradise
   That birk grew fair eneugh.

---

carline: old woman; *mirk*: dark; *birk*: birch, associated with death; *sheugh*: trench

'Blow up the fire, my maidens,
   Bring water from the well;
For a' my house shall feast this night
   Since my three sons are well.'

And she has made to them a bed,
   She's made it large and wide,
And she's taken her mantle her about,
   Sat down at the bed-side.

Up then crew the red, red cock
   Up and crew the grey;
The eldest to the youngest said,
   ''Tis time we were away.'

The cock he hadna craw'd but once
   And clapp'd his wings at a'
When the youngest to the eldest said,
   'Brother, we must awa'.

'The cock doth craw, the day doth daw,
   The channerin' worm doth chide;
Gin we be mist out o' our place
   A sair pain we maun bide.

'Fare ye weel, my mother dear;
   Fareweel to barn and byre;
And fare ye weel, the bonny lass
   That kindles my mother's fire.'

ANONYMOUS

channerin' worm: complaining [graveyard] worm

STRANGE COMPANY

A wife was sitting at her reel ae nicht;
And aye she sat, and aye she reeled, and aye she wished for company.

In cam a pair o' braid, braid soles, and sat down by the fireside;
And aye she sat, and aye she reeled, and aye she wished for company.

In cam a pair o' sma', sma' legs, and sat down on the braid, braid soles;
And aye she sat, and aye she reeled, and aye she wished for company.

In cam a pair o' sma', sma' thees, and sat down on the sma', sma' legs;
And aye she sat and aye she reeled, and aye she wished for company.

In cam a pair o' muckle, muckle hips, and sat down on the sma' sma' thees;
And aye she sat, and aye she reeled, and aye she wished for company.

In cam a sma', sma' waist, and sat down on the muckle, muckle hips;
And aye she sat, and aye she reeled, and aye she wished for company.

In cam a pair o' braid, braid shoulders, and sat down on the sma', sma' waist;
And aye she sat, and aye she reeled, and aye she wished for company.

In cam a pair o' sma', sma' arms, and sat down on the braid, braid shoulders;
And aye she sat, and aye she reeled, and aye she wished for company.

In cam a pair o' muckle, muckle hands, and sat down on the sma', sma' arms;
And aye she sat, and aye she reeled, and aye she wished for company.

In cam a sma', sma' neck, and sat down on the braid, braid shoulders;

And aye she sat, and aye she reeled, and aye she wished for company.

In cam a great big head, and sat down on the sma', sma' neck.

'What way hae ye sic braid, braid feet?' quoth the wife.
'Muckle ganging, muckle ganging.'
'What way hae ye sic sma', sma' legs?'
'*Aih-h-h!* – late – and *wee-e-e* moul.'
'What way hae ye sic big, big hips?'
'Muckle sitting, muckle sitting.'
'What way hae ye sic a sma', sma' waist?'
'*Aih-h-h!* – late – and *wee-e-e* – moul.'
'What way hae ye sic braid, braid shoulders?'
'Wi' carrying broom, wi' carrying broom.'
'What way hae ye sic sma', sma' arms?'
'*Aih-h-h!* – late and *wee-e-e* – moul.'
'What way hae ye sic muckle, muckle hands?'
'Threshing wi' an iron flail, threshing wi' an iron flail.'
'What way hae ye sic a sma', sma' neck?'
'*Aih-h-h!* – late – and *wee-e-e* moul.'
'What way hae ye sic a muckle, muckle head?'
'Muckle wit, muckle wit.'

'What do ye come for?
'For YOU!'

ANONYMOUS

thees: thighs; *muckle ganging*: much walking;
late and moul: made of graveyard dust and ashes

KILMENY RETURNS FROM THE LAND OF THE SPIRITS

When many a day had come and fled
When grief grew calm, and hope was dead.
When mass for Kilmeny's soul had been sung,
When the bedesman had pray'd and the dead bell rung.
Late, late in gloamin' when all was still,
When the fringe was red on the westlin hill,
The wood was sere, the moon i' the wane,
The reek o' the cot hung over the plain,
Like a little wee cloud in the world its lane;
When the ingle low'd wi' an eiry leme,
Late, late in the gloamin' Kilmeny came hame!

'Kilmeny, Kilmeny, where have you been?
Lang hae we sought baith holt and den;
By linn, by ford, and green-wood tree,
Yet you are halesome and fair to see.
Where gat you that joup o' the lily scheen?
That bonnie snood of the birk sae green?
And these roses, the fairest that ever were seen?
Kilmeny, Kilmeny? where have you been?'

Kilmeny look'd up with a lovely grace,
But nae smile was seen on Kilmeny's face;
As still was her look, and as still was her e'e,
As the stillness that sleeps on a waveless sea.

westlin: western; *its lane*: alone, by itself; *low'd*: flamed; *eiry leme*: eerie gleam; *linn*: waterfall; *joup*: mantle; *birk*: birch

For Kilmeny had been she knew not where,
And Kilmeny had seen what she could not declare;
Kilmeny had been where the cock never crew,
Where the rain never fell, and the wind never blew.

But it seem'd as the harp of the sky had rung,
And the airs of heaven play'd round her tongue,
When she spake of the lovely forms she had seen,
And a land where sin had never been;
A land of love and a land of light,
Withouten sun, or moon, or night;
When the river swa'd a living stream,
And the light a pure celestial beam;
The land of vision, it would seem,
A still, an everlasting dream.

JAMES HOGG (1770–1835)
From *Kilmeny*

swa'd: swelled

THE RIDER AT THE GATE

A windy night was blowing on Rome,
The cressets guttered on Caesar's home,
The fish-boats, moored at the bridge, were breaking
The rush of the river to yellow foam.

The hinges whined to the shutters shaking,
When clip-clop-clop came a horse-hoof raking
The stones of the road at Caesar's gate;
The spear-butts jarred at the guard's awaking.

'Who goes there?' said the guard at the gate.
'What is the news, that you ride so late?'
'News most pressing, that must be spoken
To Caesar alone, and that cannot wait.'

'The Caesar sleeps; you must show a token
That the news suffice that he be awoken.
What is the news, and whence do you come?
For no light cause may his sleep be broken.'

'Out of the dark of the sands I come,
From the dark of death, with news for Rome.
A word so fell that it must be uttered
Though it strike the soul of the Caesar dumb.'

Caesar turned in his bed and muttered,
With a struggle for breath the lamp-flame guttered;
Calpurnia heard her husband moan:
  'The house is falling,
The beaten men come into their own.'

'Speak your word,' said the guard at the gate;
'Yes, but bear it to Caesar straight,
Say, "Your murderer's knives are honing,
Your killer's gang is lying in wait."

'Out of the wind that is blowing and moaning,
Through the city palace and the country loaning,
I cry, "For the world's sake, Caesar, beware,
And take this warning as my atoning.

'"Beware of the Court, of the palace stair,
Of the downcast friend who speaks so fair,
Keep from the Senate, for Death is going
On many men's feet to meet you there."

'I, who am dead, have ways of knowing
Of the crop of death that the quick are sowing.
I, who was Pompey, cry it aloud
From the dark of death, from the wind blowing.

'I, who was Pompey, once was proud,
Now I lie in the sand without a shroud;
I cry to Caesar out of my pain,
"Caesar, beware, your death is vowed."'

The light grew grey on the window-pane,
The windcocks swung in a burst of rain,
The window of Caesar flung unshuttered,
The horse-hoofs died into wind again.

Caesar turned in his bed and muttered,
With a struggle for breath the lamp-flame guttered;
Calpurnia heard her husband moan:
   'The house is falling,
The beaten men come into their own.'

JOHN MASEFIELD (1878–1967)

loaning: field, common; *quick*: living

MILLER'S END

When we moved to Miller's End,
    Every afternoon at four
A thin shadow of a shade
    Quavered through the garden-door.

Dressed in black from top to toe
    And a veil about her head.
To us it seemed as though
    She came walking from the dead.

With a basket on her arm
    Through the hedge-gap she would pass,
Never a mark that we could spy
    On the flagstones or the grass.

When we told the garden-boy
    How we saw the phantom glide,
With a grin his face was bright
    As the pool he stood beside.

'That's no ghost-walk,' Billy said
    'Nor a ghost you fear to stop –
Only old Miss Wickerby
    On a short cut to the shop.'

So next day we lay in wait,
    Passed a civil time of day,
Said how pleased we were she came
    Daily down our garden way.

Suddenly her cheek it paled,
    Turned, as quick, from ice to flame.
'Tell me,' said Miss Wickerby,
'Who spoke of me, and my name?'

'Bill the garden-boy.' She sighed,
    Said, 'Of course you could not know
How he drowned – that very pool,
    A frozen winter, – long ago.'

                    CHARLES CAUSLEY (1917–)

THE SECRET BROTHER

Jack lived in the green-house
When I was six,
With glass and with tomato plants,
Not with slates and bricks.

I didn't have a brother,
Jack became mine,
Nobody could see him,
He never gave a sign.

Just beyond the rockery,
By the apple-tree,
Jack and his old mother lived,
Only for me.

With a tin telephone
Held beneath the sheet,
I would talk to Jack each night.
We would never meet.

Once my sister caught me,
Said, 'He isn't there.
Down among the flower-pots
Cramm the gardener

Is the only person.'
I said nothing, but
Let her go on talking.
Yet I moved Jack out.

He and his old mother
Did a midnight flit.
No one knew his number:
I had altered it.

Only I could see
The sagging washing-line
And my brother making
Our own secret sign.

ELIZABETH JENNINGS
(1926–)

YOU'D BETTER BELIEVE HIM

He discovered an old rocking-horse in Woolworth's,
He tried to feed it but without much luck.
So he stroked it, had a long conversation about
The trees it came from, the attics it had visited.
Tried to take it out then
But the store detective he
Called the store manager who
Called the police who in court next morning said
'He acted strangely when arrested,
His statement read simply "I believe in rocking-horses".

We have reason to believe him mad.'
'Quite so,' said the prosecution,
'Bring in the rocking-horse as evidence.'
'I'm afraid it's escaped, sir,' said the store manager,
'Left a hoof-print as evidence
On the skull of the store detective.'
'Quite so,' said the prosecution, fearful
Of the neighing
Out in the corridor.

BRIAN PATTEN (1946–)

A ROAD IN KENTUCKY

And when that ballad lady went
    to ease the lover whose life she broke,
oh surely this is the road she took,
    road all hackled through barberry fire,
through cedar and alder and sumac and thorn.

And clay stained her flounces
    and stones cut her shoes
and the road twisted on to the loveless house
    and his cornfield dying
in the scarecrow's arms.

And when she had left her lover dying
    so stark and so stark, with the Star-of-Hope
drawn over his eyes, oh this is the road
    that lady walked in the cawing light,
so dark and so dark in the briary night.

ROBERT HAYDEN (1913–80)

LITTLE ORPHANT ANNIE

Little Orphant Annie's come to our house to stay,
An' wash the cups and saucers up, an' brush the crumbs away,
An' shoo the chickens off the porch, an' dust the hearth an' sweep,
An' make the fire, an' bake the bread, an' earn her board an' keep,
An' all us other children, when the supper things is done,
We set around the kitchen fire an' has the mostest fun
A-list'nin' to the witch-tales 'at Annie tells about,
An' the Gobble-uns 'at gits you
    Ef you
        Don't
            Watch
                Out!

Wunst they wuz a little boy wouldn't say his prayers –
An' when he went to bed at night, away up stairs,
His Mammy heerd him holler, an' his Daddy heerd him bawl,
An' when they turnt the kivvers down, he wuzn't there at all!
An' they seeked him in the rafter-room, an' cubby-hole an' press,
An' seeked him up the chimbly-flue, an' ever'wheres, I guess,
But all they ever found wuz thist his pants an' roundabout –
An' the Gobble-uns'll git you
    Ef you
        Don't
            Watch
                Out!

kivvers: bedclothes;   *roundabout*: short jacket

An' one time a little girl 'ud allus laugh an' grin,
An' make fun of ever' one, an' all her blood an' kin;
An' wunst, when they was 'company', an' ole folks wuz there,
She mocked 'em an' shocked 'em, an' said she didn't care!
An' thist as she kicked her heels, an' turn't to run an' hide,
They wuz two great Blacks Things a-standin' by her side,
An' they snatched her through the ceilin' 'fore she knowed what she's about!
An' the Gobble-uns'll git you
    Ef you
        Don't
            Watch
                Out!

An' little Orphant Annie says, when the blaze is blue,
An' the lamp-wick sputters, an' the wind goes *woo-oo*!
An' you hear the crickets quit, an' the moon is gray,
An' the lightnin'-bugs in dew is all squenched away, –
You better mind yer parents, an' yer teachurs fond an' dear,
An' churish them 'at loves you, an' dry the orphant's tear,
And he'p the pore an' needy ones 'at clusters all about,
Er the Gobble-uns'll git you
    Ef you
        Don't
            Watch
                Out!

JAMES WHITCOMB RILEY
(1849–1916)

Music and dancing

HOW SWEET THE MOONLIGHT SLEEPS

How sweet the moonlight sleeps upon this bank!
Here will we sit, and let the sounds of music
Creep in our ears: soft stillness and the night
Become the touches of sweet harmony.
Sit, Jessica. Look how the floor of heaven
Is thick inlaid with patines of bright gold:
There's not the smallest orb which thou behold'st
But in his motion like an angel sings,
Still quiring to the young-eyed cherubins;
Such harmony is in immortal souls;
But whilst this muddy vesture of decay
Doth grossly close it in, we cannot hear it.

WILLIAM SHAKESPEARE
(1564–1616)
The Merchant of Venice, V i

From COMUS

The Star that bids the Shepherd fold,
Now the top of Heav'n doth hold.
And the gilded Car of Day,
His glowing Axle doth allay
In the steep Atlantick stream,
And the slope Sun his upward beam
Shoots against the dusky Pole,
Pacing toward the other goal

Of his Chamber in the East.
Meanwhile welcome Joy, and Feast,
Midnight shout, and revelry,
Tipsy dance, and Jollity.
Braid your Locks with rosy Twine
Dropping odours, dropping Wine.
Rigour now is gone to bed,
And Advice with scrupulous head,
Strict Age, and sour Severity,
With their grave Saws in slumber lie.
We that are of purer fire
Imitate the Starry Quire,
Who in their nightly watchful Spheres,
Lead in swift round the Months and Years.
The Sounds, and Seas with all their finny drove
Now to the Moon in wavering Morris move,
And on the Tawny Sands and Shelves,
Trip the pert Fairies and the dapper Elves;
By dimpled Brook, and Fountain brim,
The Wood-Nymphs decked with Daisies trim,
Their merry wakes and pastimes keep:
What hath night to do with sleep?
Night hath better sweets to prove,
Venus now wakes, and wak'ns Love . . .
Come, knit hands, and beat the ground,
In a light fantastic round.

JOHN MILTON (1608–74)

From A SONG FOR ST CECILIA'S DAY

What passion cannot Music raise and quell?
    When Jubal struck the chorded shell
       His listening brethren stood around,
    And, wondering, on their faces fell
       To worship that celestial sound:
Less than a God they thought there could not dwell
      Within the hollow of that shell,
    That spoke so sweetly, and so well.
What passion cannot Music raise and quell?

    The trumpet's loud clangour
       Excites us to arms
    With shrill notes of anger
       And mortal alarms.
    The double double double beat
      Of the thundering drum
      Cries, Hark! the foes come;
Charge, charge, 'tis too late to retreat!

    The soft complaining flute,
    In dying notes, discovers
    The woes of hopeless lovers,
Whose dirge is whisper'd by the warbling lute.

    Sharp violins proclaim
   Their jealous pangs and desperation,
   Fury, frantic indignation,
   Depth of pains, and height of passion,
     For the fair, disdainful dame.

But O, what art can teach
What human voice can reach,
   The sacred organ's praise?
Notes inspiring holy love,
Notes that wing their heavenly ways
To mend the choirs above.

Orpheus could lead the savage race;
And trees unrooted left their place,
   Sequacious of the lyre;
But bright Cecilia rais'd the wonder higher:
When to her organ vocal breath was given,
   An angel heard, and straight appear'd
   Mistaking Earth for Heaven.

JOHN DRYDEN (1631–1700)

HYMN OF PAN

From the forests and highlands
   We come, we come;
From the river-girt islands,
   Where loud waves are dumb,
Listening to my sweet pipings.
   The wind in the reeds and the rushes,
     The bees on the bells of thyme,
   The birds in the myrtle bushes,
     The cicale above in the lime,
And the lizards below in the grass,
Were as silent as ever old Tmolus was,
   Listening to my sweet pipings.

Liquid Peneus was flowing,
    And all dark Tempe lay
In Pelion's shadow, outgrowing
    The light of the dying day,
Speeded by my sweet pipings.
    The Sileni and Sylvans and Fauns,
        And the Nymphs of the woods and waves,
    To the edge of the moist river-lawns,
        And the brink of the dewy caves,
And all that did then attend and follow,
Were silent with love, as you now, Apollo,
    With envy of my sweet pipings.

I sang of the dancing stars,
    I sang of the daedal earth,
And of heaven, and the giant wars,
    And love, and death, and birth.
And then I changed my pipings –
    Singing how down the vale of Maenalus
        I pursued a maiden, and clasp'd a reed:
    Gods and men, we are all deluded thus;
        It breaks in our bosom, and then we bleed.
All wept – as I think both ye now would,
If envy or age had not frozen your blood –
    At the sorrow of my sweet pipings.

                        PERCY BYSSHE SHELLEY
                        (1792–1822)

THE SPLENDOUR FALLS ON CASTLE WALLS

    The splendour falls on castle walls
        And snowy summits old in story:
    The long light shakes across the lakes,
        And the wild cataract leaps in glory.
Blow, bugle, blow, set the wild echoes flying,
Blow, bugle; answer, echoes, dying, dying, dying.

    O hark, O hear! how thin and clear,
        And thinner, clearer, farther going!
    O sweet and far from cliff and scar
        The horns of Elfland faintly blowing!
Blow, let us hear the purple glens replying:
Blow, bugle; answer, echoes, dying, dying, dying.

    O love, they die in yon rich sky,
        They faint on hill or field or river;
    Our echoes roll from soul to soul,
        And grow for ever and for ever.
Blow, bugle, blow, set the wild echoes flying,
And answer, echoes, answer, dying, dying, dying.

                ALFRED,
                LORD TENNYSON (1809–92)

                From *The Princess*

THE MOCK TURTLE'S SONG

'Will you walk a little faster,' said a whiting to a snail,
'There's a porpoise close behind me, and he's treading on my tail.
See how eagerly the lobsters and the turtles all advance!
They are waiting on the shingle – will you come and join the dance?
   Will you, won't you, will you, won't you, will you join the dance?
   Will you, won't you, will you, won't you, won't you join the dance?

'You can really have no notion how delightful it will be
When they take us up and throw us, with the lobsters, out to sea!'
But the snail replied 'Too far, too far!' and gave a look askance –
Said he thanked the whiting kindly, but he would not join the dance.
   Would not, could not, would not, could not, would not join the dance.
   Would not, could not, would not, could not, could not join the dance.

'What matters it how far we go?' his scaly friend replied.
'There is another shore, you know, upon the other side.
The further off from England the nearer is to France –
Then turn not pale, beloved snail, but come and join the dance.
   Will you, won't you, will you, won't you, will you join the dance?
   Will you, won't you, will you, won't you, won't you join the dance?'

LEWIS CARROLL (1832–98)

From *Alice's Adventures in Wonderland*

THE FIDDLER OF DOONEY

When I play on my fiddle in Dooney
Folk dance like a wave of the sea;
My cousin is priest in Kilvarnet,
My brother in Mocharabuiee.

I passed my brother and cousin:
They read in their books of prayer;
I read in my book of songs
I bought at the Sligo fair.

When we come at the end of time
To Peter sitting in state,
He will smile on the three old spirits,
But call me first through the gate;

For the good are always the merry,
Save by an evil chance,
And the merry love the fiddle,
And the merry love to dance:

And when the folk there spy me,
They will all come up to me,
With 'Here is the fiddler of Dooney!'
And dance like a wave of the sea.

                    W.B. YEATS (1865–1939)

THE TALKING DRUMS

I hear the beat
Of the drums
The Atumpan drums.
Asante Kotpko:
Kum-apem-a-apem-beba!

I hear the beat
Of Prempeh drums,
Osei Tutu drums.

I hear the call
Of Nnawuta:
Tin-tinn konn-konn!
Tinn-tinn konn-konn!
Konn-konn!
I ponder the valour
Of the mourned and mighty
African might.
I sense the resonance
Of Dawuro beats:
Tonn-tonn sann-sann!
Tonn-tonn sann-sann!
Sann-sann!

I muse upon Ghana,
Melle and Songhey.
I hear the echo
Of Fontomfro,
The beat of
Mpintin drums:
Damirifa due ... due!
Damirifi due ... due!
Damirifi ooo-oo-o!

And *ooo*! The Sage!
Ankoanna Osagyefo
Bringing up the rear
At shoulders' acclaim:
The Sage who notched
Beauty and splendour
On Africa's glory!

I hear the beat
Of the drums!
I hear the beat
Of the Talking Drums!

     KOJO GYINAYE KYEI

DANSE AFRICAINE

The low beating of the tom-toms,
The slow beating of the tom-toms,
 Low . . . slow
 Slow . . . low –
 Stir your blood.
  Dance!
A night-veiled girl
 Whirls softly into a
 Circle of light.
 Whirls softly . . . slowly,
Like a wisp of smoke around the fire –

> And the tom-toms beat
> And the tom-toms beat,
> And the low beating of the tom-toms
> > Stirs your blood.

LANGSTON HUGHES
(1902–67)

TARANTELLA

Do you remember an Inn,
Miranda?
Do you remember an Inn?
And the tedding and the spreading
Of the straw for a bedding,
And the fleas that tease in the High Pyrenees,
And the wine that tasted of the tar?
And the cheers and the jeers of the young muleteers
(Under the dark of the vine verandah)?
Do you remember an Inn, Miranda,
Do you remember an Inn?
And the cheers and the jeers of the young muleteers
Who hadn't got a penny,
And who weren't paying any,
And the hammer at the doors and the Din?
And the Hip! Hop! Hap!
Of the clap
Of the hands to the twirl and the swirl
Of the girl gone chancing,
Glancing,
Dancing,
    Backing and advancing,

Snapping of the clapper to the spin
Out and in –
And the Ting, Tong, Tang of the Guitar!
Do you remember an Inn,
Miranda?
Do you remember an Inn?

    Never more;
       Miranda,
       Never more.
       Only the high peaks hoar;
       And Aragon a torrent at the door.
       No sound
       In the walls of the Halls where falls
       The tread of the dead to the ground.
       No sound:
       Only the boom
       Of the far Waterfall like Doom.

HILAIRE BELLOC (1870–1953)

POLKA

'Tra la la la –
   See me dance the polka,'
Said Mr Wagg like a bear,
'With my top hat
And my whiskers that –
(Tra la la la) trap the Fair.

Where the waves seem chiming haycocks
I dance the polka; there
Stand Venus' children in their gay frocks –
Maroon and marine – and stare

To see me fire my pistol
Through the distance blue as my coat;
Like Wellington, Byron, the Marquis of Bristol,
Buzbied great trees float.

While the wheezing hurdy-gurdy
Of the marine wind blows me
To the tune of Annie Rooney, sturdy,
O'er the sheafs of the sea;

And bright as a seedsman's packet
With zinnias, candytufts chill,
Is Mrs Marigold's jacket
As she gapes at the inn door still,

Where at dawn in the box of the sailor,
Blue as the decks of the sea,
Nelson awoke, crowed like the cocks,
Then back to dust sank he.

   And Robinson Crusoe
   Rues so
   The bright and foxy beer –
   But he finds fresh isles in a negress' smiles –
The poxy doxy dear,

As they watch me dance the polka,'
Said Mr Wagg like a bear,
'In my top hat and my whiskers that –
Tra la la la, trap the Fair.

Tra la la la –
Tra la la la –
Tra la la la la la la la
    La
    La
    La!'

          EDITH SITWELL (1887–1964)

LORD OF THE DANCE

I danced in the morning
When the world was begun,
And I danced on the moon
And the stars and the sun,
And I came down from heaven
And I danced on the earth,
At Bethlehem,
I had my birth.
 Dance then, wherever you may be,
 I am the Lord of the Dance, said he,
 And I'll lead you all wherever you may be,
 And I'll lead you all in the dance, said he.

I danced for the scribe
And the pharisee,
They would not dance
And they would not follow me.
I danced for the fishermen,
For James and John,
They came with me
And the dance went on.

I danced on a Friday
When the sky turned black –
It's hard to dance
With the devil on your back.
They buried my body
And they thought I'd gone,
But I am the dance
And I still go on.

They cut me down
And I leap up high:
I am the life
That'll never, never die;
I'll live in you
If you'll live in me –
I am the Lord
Of the Dance said he.

      SYDNEY CARTER (1915-)

Battles, soldiers and patriots

WAR SONG OF THE SARACENS

We are they who come faster than fate: we are they who ride early
                                                                             or late:
We storm at your ivory gate: Pale Kings of the Sunset, beware!
Not on silk nor in samet we lie, not in curtained solemnity die
Among women who chatter and cry, and children who mumble a prayer.
But we sleep by the ropes of the camp, and we rise with a shout,
                                                                   and we tramp
With the sun or the moon for a lamp, and the spray of the wind in
                                                                         our hair.

From the lands, where the elephants are, to the forts of Merou and
                                                                         Balghar,
Our steel we have brought and our star to shine on the ruins of Rûm.
We have marched from the Indus to Spain, and by God we will go
                                                                       there again;
We have stood on the shore of the plain where the Waters of
                                                                   Destiny boom.
A mart of destruction we made at Jalula where men were afraid,
For death was a difficult trade, and the sword was a broker of doom;

And the Spear was a Desert Physician who cured not a few of ambition,
And drave not a few to perdition with medicine bitter and strong:
And the shield was a grief to the fool and as bright as a desolate pool,
And as straight as the rock of Stamboul when their cavalry
                                                                   thundered along:
For the coward was drowned with the brave when our battle
                                                             sheered up like a wave,
And the dead to the desert we gave, and the glory of God in our song.

                                                  JAMES ELROY FLECKER
                                                  (1884–1915)

THE DESTRUCTION OF SENNACHERIB

The Assyrian came down like the wolf on the fold,
And his cohorts were gleaming in purple and gold;
And the sheen of their spears was like stars on the sea,
When the blue wave rolls nightly on deep Galilee.

Like the leaves of the forest when Summer is green,
That host with their banners at sunset were seen;
Like the leaves of the forest when Autumn hath blown,
That host on the morrow lay wither'd and strown.

For the Angel of Death spread his wings on the blast,
And breathed in the face of the foe as he pass'd;
And the eyes of the sleepers wax'd deadly and chill,
    And their hearts but once heaved, and for ever grew still!

And there lay the steed with his nostril all wide,
But through it there roll'd not the breath of his pride;
And the foam of his gasping lay white on the turf,
And cold as the spray of the rock-beating surf.

And there lay the rider distorted and pale,
With the dew on his brow, and the rust on his mail:
And the tents were all silent, the banners alone,
The lances uplifted, the trumpet unblown.

And the widows of Ashur are loud in their wail
And the idols are broke in the temple of Baal;
And the might of the Gentile, unsmote by the sword,
Hath melted like snow in the glance of the Lord!

                              GEORGE GORDON,
                              LORD BYRON (1788–1824)

PIBROCH OF DONUIL DHU

Pibroch of Donuil Dhu,
  Pibroch of Donuil,
Wake thy wild voice anew,
  Summon Clan-Conuil.
Come away, come away,
  Hark to the summons!
Come in your war array,
  Gentles and commons.

Come from deep glen, and
  From mountain so rocky,
The war-pipe and pennon
  Are at Inverlochy.
Come every hill-plaid, and
  True heart that wears one,
Come every steel blade, and
  Strong hand that bears one.

Leave untended the herd,
  The flock without shelter;
Leave the corpse uninterr'd,
  The bride at the altar;
Leave the deer, leave the steer,
  Leave nets and barges;
Come with your fighting gear,
  Broadswords and targes.

Come as the winds come, when
  Forests are rended,
Come as the waves come, when
  Navies are stranded:

> Faster come, faster come,
>   Faster and faster,
> Chief, vassal, page and groom,
>   Tenant and master.
>
> Fast they come, fast they come;
>   See how they gather!
> Wide waves the eagle plume,
>   Blended with heather.
> Cast your plaids, draw your blades,
>   Forward, each man, set!
> Pibroch of Donuil Dhu,
>   Knell for the onset!

SIR WALTER SCOTT
(1771–1832)

A pibroch is a tune with variations, played by bagpipes; here martial music.

A JACOBITE'S EPITAPH

To my true king I offer'd free from stain
Courage and faith; vain faith, and courage vain.
For him I threw lands, honours, wealth, away,
And one dear hope, that was more prized than they.
For him I languish'd in a foreign clime,
Gray-hair'd with sorrow in my manhood's prime;
Heard on Lavernia Scargill's whispering trees,
And pined by Arno for my lovelier Tees;
Beheld each night my home in fever'd sleep,
Each morning started from the dream to weep;
Till God, who saw me tried too sorely, gave
The resting-place I ask'd, an early grave.
O thou, whom chance leads to this nameless stone
From that proud country which was once mine own.
By those white cliffs I never more must see,
By that dear language which I spake like thee,
Forget all feuds, and shed one English tear
O'er English dust. A broken heart lies here.

THOMAS BABINGTON,
LORD MACAULAY (1800–59)

THE PATRIOT

It was roses, roses all the way,
   With myrtle mixed in my path like mad:
The house-roofs seemed to heave and sway,
   The church-spires flamed, such flags they had,
A year ago on this very day!

The air broke into a mist with bells,
   The old walls rocked with the crowd and cries.
Had I said, 'Good folk, mere noise repels –
   But give me your sun from yonder skies!'
They had answered, 'And afterward, what else?'

Alack, it was I who leaped at the sun
   To give it my loving friends to keep!
Nought man could do, have I left undone:
   And you see my harvest, what I reap
This very day, now a year is run.

There's nobody on the house-tops now –
   Just a palsied few at the windows set;
For the best of the sight is, all allow,
   At the Shambles' Gate or, better yet,
By the very scaffold's foot, I trow.

I go in the rain, and, more than needs,
   A rope cuts both my wrists behind;
And I think, by the feel, my forehead bleeds,
   For they fling, whoever has a mind,
Stones at me for my year's misdeeds.

Thus I entered, and thus I go!
   In triumphs, people have dropped down dead.
'Paid by the world, – what dost thou owe
   Me?' God might question: now instead,
'Tis God shall repay! I am safer so.

ROBERT BROWNING (1812–89

A ST HELENA LULLABY

How far is St Helena from a little child at play?
   What makes you want to wander there with all the world between?
Oh Mother, call your son again or else he'll run away,
   (*No one thinks of winter when the grass is green!*)

How far is St Helena from a fight in Paris street?
   I haven't time to answer now – the men are falling fast.
The guns begin to thunder, and the drums begin to beat.
   (*If you take the first step you will take the last!*)

How far is St Helena from the field of Austerlitz?
   You couldn't hear me if I told you – so loud the cannons roar.
But not so far for people who are living by their wits.
   (*'Gay go up' means 'gay go down' the wide world o'er!*)

How far is St Helena from an Emperor of France?
   I cannot see – I cannot tell – the crowns they dazzle so.
The Kings sit down to dinner, and the Queens stand up to dance.
   (*After open weather you may look for snow!*)

How far is St Helena from the Capes of Trafalgar?
    A longish way – a longish way – with ten year more to run.
It's South across the water underneath a setting star.
    (*What you cannot finish you must leave undone!*)

How far is St Helena from the Beresina ice?
    An ill way – a chill way – the ice begins to crack.
But not so far for gentlemen who never took advice.
    (*When you can't go forward you must e'en come back!*)

How far is St Helena from the field of Waterloo?
    A near way – a clear way – the ship will take you soon.
A pleasant place for gentlemen with little left to do.
    (*Morning never tries you till the afternoon!*)

How far from St Helena to the Gate of Heaven's Grace?
    That no one knows – that no one knows – and no one ever will.
But fold your hands across your heart and cover up your face,
    And after all your trapesings, child, lie still!

RUDYARD KIPLING
(1865–1936)

THE EVE OF WATERLOO

There was a sound of revelry by night,
And Belgium's capital had gathered then
Her Beauty and her Chivalry, and bright
The lamps shone o'er fair women and brave men,
A thousand hearts beat happily; and when
Music arose with its voluptuous swell,
Soft eyes looked love to eyes which spake again,
And all went merry as a marriage bell;
But hush! hark! a deep sound strikes like a rising knell!

Did ye not hear it? – No; 'twas but the wind,
Or the car rattling o'er the stony street;
On with the dance! let joy be unconfined;
No sleep till morn, when Youth and Pleasure meet
To chase the glowing hours with flying feet –
But hark! – that heavy sound breaks in once more,
As if the clouds its echo would repeat;
And nearer, clearer, deadlier than before!
Arm! Arm! it is – it is – the cannon's opening roar!

* * *

Ah! then and there was hurrying to and fro,
And gathering tears, and tremblings of distress,
And cheeks all pale, which but an hour ago
Blushed at the praise of their own loveliness;
And there were sudden partings, such as press
The life from out young hearts, and choking sighs
Which ne'er might be repeated; who could guess
If ever more should meet those mutual eyes,
Since upon night so sweet such awful morn could rise!

And there was mounting in hot haste: the steed,
The mustering squadron, and the clattering car,
Went pouring forward with impetuous speed,
And swiftly forming in the ranks of war;
And the deep thunder peal on peal afar;
And near, the beat of the alarming drum
Roused up the soldier ere the morning star;
While thronged the citizens with terror dumb,
Or whispering, with white lips – 'The foe! they come!
                                                they come!'

And wild and high the 'Cameron's gathering' rose!
The war-note of Lochiel, which Albyn's hills
Have heard, and heard, too, have her Saxon foes:–
How in the noon of night that pibroch thrills,
Savage and shrill! But with the breath which fills
Their mountain-pipe, so fill the mountaineers
With the fierce native daring which instils
The stirring memory of a thousand years,
And Evan's, Donald's fame rings in each clansman's ears!

And Ardennes waves above them her green leaves,
Dewy with nature's tear-drops as they pass,
Grieving, if aught inanimate e'er grieves,
Over the unreturning brave, – alas!
Ere evening to be trodden like the grass
Which now beneath them, but above shall grow
In its next verdure, when this fiery mass
Of living valour, rolling on the foe,
And burning with high hopes shall moulder cold and low.

Last noon beheld them full of lusty life,
Last eve in Beauty's circle proudly gay,
The midnight brought the signal-sound of strife,
The morn the marshalling in arms, – the day
Battle's magnificently stern array!
The thunder-clouds close o'er it, which when rent
The earth is covered thick with other clay,
Which her own clay shall cover, heaped and pent,
Rider and horse, – friend and foe, – in one red burial blent!

GEORGE GORDON,
LORD BYRON (1788–1824)

From *Childe Harold's Pilgrimage*

NAPOLEON'S FAREWELL

Farewell to the Land where the gloom of my glory
Arose and o'ershadowed the earth with her name –
She abandons me now – but the page of her story,
The brightest and blackest, is fill'd with my fame.
I have warred with a world which vanquished me only
When the meteor of Conquest allured me too far;
I have coped with the nations which dread me thus lonely,
The last single Captive to millions in war.

Farewell to thee, France! when thy diadem crowned me,
I made thee the gem and the wonder of earth,
But thy weakness decrees I should leave as I found thee,
Decayed in thy glory, and sunk in thy worth.
Oh! for the veteran hearts that were wasted
In strife with the storm, when their battles were won –
Then the Eagle, whose gaze in that moment was blasted,
Had still soared with eyes fixed on victory's sun!

Farewell to thee, France! but when Liberty rallies
Once more in thy regions, remember me then, –
The violet still grows in the depth of thy valleys;
Though withered, thy tears will unfold it again –
Yet, yet, I may baffle the hosts that surround us,
And yet may thy heart leap awake to my voice –
There are links which must break in the chain that has bound us,
Then turn thee and call on the Chief of thy choice!

GEORGE GORDON,
LORD BYRON (1788–1824)

O CAPTAIN! MY CAPTAIN!

O Captain! my Captain! our fearful trip is done,
The ship has weather'd every rack, the prize we sought is won,
The port is near, the bells I hear, the people all exulting,
While follow eyes the steady keel, the vessel grim and daring;
   But O heart! heart! heart!
     O the bleeding drops of red,
       Where on the deck my Captain lies,
         Fallen cold and dead.

O Captain! my Captain! rise up and hear the bells;
Rise up – for you the flag is flung – for you the bugle trills,
For you bouquets and ribbon'd wreaths – for you the shores a-crowding,
For you they call, the swaying mass, their eager faces turning;
   Here Captain! dear father!
     This arm beneath your head!
       It is some dream that on the deck,
         You've fallen cold and dead.

My Captain does not answer, his lips are pale and still,
My father does not feel my arm, he has no pulse nor will,
The ship is anchor'd safe and sound, its voyage closed and done,
From fearful trip the victor ship comes in with object won;
    Exult, O shores, and ring, O bells!
      But I, with mournful tread,
        Walk the deck my Captain lies,
          Fallen cold and dead.

                        WALT WHITMAN (1819–92)

TOMMY

I went into a public-'ouse to get a pint o' beer,
The publican 'e up an' sez, 'We serve no red-coats here.'
The girls be'ind the bar they laughed an' giggled fit to die,
I outs into the streets again an' to myself sez I:
    O it's Tommy this, an' Tommy that, an' 'Tommy, go away';
    But it's 'Thank you, Mister Atkins,' when the band begins to play –
    The band begins to play, my boys, the band begins to play,
    O it's 'Thank you, Mister Atkins,' when the band begins to play.

I went into a theatre as sober as could be,
They gave a drunk civilian room, but 'adn't none for me;
They sent me to the gallery or round the music-'alls,
But when it comes to fightin', Lord! they'll shove me in the stalls!
    For it's Tommy this, an' Tommy that, an' 'Tommy, wait outside';
    But it's 'Special train for Atkins' when the trooper's on the tide –
    The troopship's on the tide, my boys, the troopship's on the tide,
    O it's 'Special train for Atkins' when the trooper's on the tide.

Yes, makin' mock o' uniforms that guard you while you sleep
Is cheaper than them uniforms, an' they're starvation cheap;
An' hustlin' drunken soldiers when they're goin' large a bit
Is five times better business than paradin' in full kit.
    Then it's Tommy this, an' Tommy that, and 'Tommy, 'ow's yer soul?'
    But it's 'Thin red line of 'eroes' when the drums begin to roll,
    The drums begin to roll, my boys, the drums begin to roll,
    O, it's 'Thin red line of 'eroes' when the drums begin to roll.

We aren't no thin red 'eroes, nor we aren't no blackguards too,
But single men in barricks, most remarkable like you;
An' if sometimes our conduck isn't all your fancy paints,
Why, single men in barricks don't grow into plaster saints;
    While it's Tommy this, an' Tommy that, an' 'Tommy, fall be'ind,'
    But it's 'Please to walk in front, sir,' when there's trouble in the wind –
    There's trouble in the wind, my boys, there's trouble in the wind,
    O it's 'Please to walk in front, sir,' when there's trouble in the wind.

You talk o' better food for us, an' schools, an' fires, an' all:
We'll wait for extry rations if you treat us rational.
Don't mess about the cook-room slops, but prove it to our face
The Widow's Uniform is not the soldier-man's disgrace.
    For it's Tommy this, an' Tommy that, an' 'Chuck him out, the brute!'
    But it's 'Saviour of 'is country' when the guns begin to shoot;
    An' it's Tommy this, an' Tommy that, an' anything you please;
    An' Tommy ain't a bloomin' fool – you bet that Tommy sees!

                              RUDYARD KIPLING
                                  (1865–1936)

Thomas Atkins: private soldier; *the Widow*: Queen Victoria

ANTHEM FOR DOOMED YOUTH

What passing-bells for these who die as cattle?
    Only the monstrous anger of the guns.
    Only the stuttering rifles' rapid rattle
Can patter out their hasty orisons.
    No mockeries for them from prayers or bells,
    Nor any voice of mourning save the choirs –
    The shrill, demented choirs of wailing shells;
And bugles calling for them from sad shires.

What candles may be held to speed them all?
    Not in the hands of boys, but in their eyes
Shall shine the holy glimmers of good-byes.
    The pallor of girls' brows shall be their pall;
Their flowers the tenderness of silent minds,
And each slow dusk a drawing-down of blinds.

                          WILFRED OWEN (1893–1918)

EPITAPHS ON THE WAR: THE COWARD

I could not look on Death, which being known,
Men led me to him, blindfold and alone.

                          RUDYARD KIPLING
                          (1865–1936)

(The punishment for cowardice in battle is death by a firing squad.)

DISABLED

He sat in a wheeled chair, waiting for dark,
And shivered in his ghastly suit of grey,
Legless, sewn short at elbow. Through the park
Voices of boys rang saddening like a hymn,
Voices of play and pleasure after day,
Till gathering sleep had mothered them from him.

About this time Town used to swing so gay
When glow-lamps budded in the light blue trees,
And girls glanced lovelier as the air grew dim, –
In the old times, before he threw away his knees.
Now he will never feel again how slim
Girls' waists are, or how warm their subtle hands;
All of them touch him like some queer disease.

There was an artist silly for his face,
For it was younger than his youth, last year.
Now, he is old; his back will never brace;
He's lost his colour very far from here,
Poured it down shell-holes till the veins ran dry,
And half his lifetime lapsed in the hot race
And leap of purple spurted from his thigh.
One time he liked a blood-smear down his leg,
After the matches, carried shoulder-high.
It was after football, when he'd drunk a peg,
He thought he'd better join. – He wonders why.
Someone had said he'd look a god in kilts,
That's why; and maybe, too, to please his Meg;
Aye, that was it, to please the giddy jilts
He asked to join. He didn't have to beg;
Smiling they wrote his lie; aged nineteen years.

Germans he scarcely thought of; all their guilt
And Austria's, did not move him. And no fears
Of Fear came yet. He thought of jewelled hilts
For daggers in plaid socks; of smart salutes;
And care of arms; and leave; and pay arrears;
Esprit de corps; and hints for young recruits.
And soon, he was drafted out with drums and cheers.

Some cheered him home, but not as crowds cheer Goal.
Only a solemn man who brought him fruits
Thanked him; and then inquired about his soul.

Now, he will spend a few sick years in institutes,
And do what things the rules consider wise,
And take whatever pity they may dole.
Tonight he noticed how the women's eyes
Passed from him to the strong men that were whole.
How cold and late it is! Why don't they come
And put him into bed? Why don't they come?

        WILFRED OWEN (1893–1918)

Birds and beasts

THE CUCKOO IS A MERRY BIRD

The cuckoo is a merry bird,
She sings as she flies,
She brings us glad tidings
And tells us no lies.

She sucks the birds' eggs
To make her voice clear,
And the more she cries 'Cuckoo'
The summer draws near.

The cuckoo is a lazy bird,
She never builds a nest,
She makes herself busy
By singing to the rest.

She never hatches her own young,
And that we all know,
But leaves it for some other bird
While she cries 'Cuckoo'.

And when her time is come
Her voice we no longer hear,
And where she goes we do not know
Until another year.

The cuckoo comes in April,
She sings a song in May,
In June she beats upon the drum,
And then she'll fly away.

ANONYMOUS

beat upon the drum: when the cuckoo changes its tune to Cuck-cuck

CUCKOO, CUCKOO

Cuckoo, Cuckoo,
What do you do?

In April
I open my bill.

In May
I sing night and day.

In June
I change my tune.

In July
Away I fly.

In August
Go I must.

ANONYMOUS

SWEET SUFFOLK OWL

Sweet Suffolk owl, so trimly dight
With feathers like a lady bright,
Thou singest alone, sitting by night,
Te whit, te whoo, te whit, te whit.
Thy note, that forth so freely rolls,
With shrill command the mouse controls,
And sings a dirge for dying souls,
Te whit, te whoo, te whit, te whit.

ANONYMOUS

Madrigal from Thomas Vautor: *The First Set*, 1619

dight: adorned

THE OWL

When cats run home and light is come,
    And dew is cold upon the ground,
And the far-off stream is dumb,
    And the whirring sail goes round,
    And the whirring sail goes round;
      Alone and warming his five wits,
      The white owl in the belfry sits.

When merry milkmaids click the latch,
  And rarely smells the new-mown hay,
And the cock hath sung beneath the thatch
  Twice or thrice his roundelay,
  Twice or thrice his roundelay:
    Alone and warming his five wits,
    The white owl in the belfry sits.

ALFRED,
LORD TENNYSON (1809–92)

AUTUMN BIRDS

The wild duck startles like a sudden thought,
And heron slow as if it might be caught.
The flopping crows on weary wings go by
And grey beard jackdaws noising as they fly.
The crowds of starnels whizz and hurry by,
And darken like a cloud the evening sky.
The larks like thunder rise and suthy round,
Then drop and nestle in the stubble ground.
The wild swan hurries high and noises loud
With white neck peering to the evening cloud.
The weary rooks to distant woods are gone.
With lengths of tail the magpie winnows on
To neighbouring tree, and leaves the distant crow
While small birds nestle in the hedge below.

JOHN CLARE (1793–1864)

starnel: starling; *suthy*: make a rushing sound; *winnow*: beat the air

THE SANDPIPER

Across the lonely beach we flit,
    One little sandpiper and I;
And fast I gather, bit by bit,
    The scattered driftwood, bleached and dry.
The wild waves reach their hands for it,
    The wild wind raves, the tide runs high,
As up and down the beach we flit –
    One little sandpiper and I.

Above our heads the sullen clouds
    Scud black and swift across the sky;
Like silent ghosts in misty shrouds
    Stand out the white lighthouses high.
Almost as far as eye can reach
    I see the close-reefed vessels fly,
As fast we flit along the beach –
    One little sandpiper and I.

I watch him as he skims along
    Uttering his sweet and mournful cry;
He starts not at my fitful song
    Or flash of fluttering drapery.
He has no thought of any wrong,
    He scans me with a fearless eye;
Staunch friends are we, well-tried and strong,
    The little sandpiper and I.

Comrade, where wilt thou be tonight
    When the loosed storm breaks furiously?
My driftwood fire will burn so bright!
    To what warm shelter canst thou fly?

I do not fear for thee, though wroth
   The tempest rushes through the sky:
For are we not God's children both,
   Thou, little sandpiper, and I?

CELIA THAXTER (1835–94)

CROWS

I like to walk
And hear the black crows talk.

I like to lie
And watch crows sail the sky.

I like the crow
That wants the wind to blow:

I like the one
That thinks the wind is fun.

I like to see,
Crows spilling from a tree,

And try to find
The top crow left behind.

I like to hear
Crows caw that spring is near.

I like the great
Wild clamour of crow hate

Three farms away
When owls are out by day.

I like the slow,
Tired homeward-flying crow;

I like the sight
Of crows for my good night.

                DAVID McCORD (1897-)

THE EAGLE

He clasps the crag with crooked hands;
Close to the sea in lonely lands,
Ring'd with the azure world, he stands.

The wrinkled sea beneath him crawls;
He watches from his mountain walls,
And like a thunderbolt he falls.

                ALFRED,
                LORD TENNYSON (1809–92)

THE SPIDER

The spider holds a silver ball
In unperceived hands –
    And dancing softly to himself
His yarn of pearl – unwinds.

He plies from nought to nought –
In unsubstantial trade –
Supplants our tapestries with his –
In half the period.

An hour to rear supreme
His continents of light –
Then dangle from the housewife's broom –
His boundaries – forgot.

EMILY DICKINSON (1830–86)

THE VIXEN

Among the taller wood with ivy hung
The old fox plays and dances round her young.
She snuffs and barks if any passes by
And swings her tail and turns prepared to fly.
The horseman hurries by, she bolts to see
And turns again, from danger never free.
If any stands she runs among the poles
And barks and snaps and drives them in the holes.
The shepherd sees them and the boy goes by
And gets a stick and progs the hole to try.
They get all still and lie in safety sure,
And out again when everything's secure,
And start and snap at blackbirds bouncing by
To fight and catch the great white butterfly.

JOHN CLARE (1793–1864)

prog: prod

HARES AT PLAY

The birds are gone to bed, the cows are still
And sheep lie panting on each old mole hill
And underneath the willow's grey-green bough
Like toil a-resting – lies the fallow plough.
The timid hares throw daylight's fears away
On the lane's road to dust, and dance and play,
Then dabble in the grain by nought deterred
To lick the dewfall from the barley's beard.
Then out they sturt again and round the hill
Like happy thoughts – dance – squat – and loiter still.
Till milking maidens in the early morn
Jingle their yokes and sturt them in the corn.
Through well known beaten paths each nimbling hare
Sturts quick as fear – and seeks its hidden lair.

JOHN CLARE (1793–1864)

sturt: startle, or move suddenly

HEDGEHOG

Twitching the leaves just where the drainpipe clogs
In ivy leaves and mud, a purposeful
Creature about its business. Dogs
Fear his stiff seriousness. He chews away

At beetles, worms, slugs, frogs. Can kill a hen
With one snap of his jaws, can taunt a snake
To death on muscled spines. Old countrymen
Tell tales of hedgehogs sucking a cow dry.

But this one, cramped by houses, fences, walls,
Must have slept here all winter in that heap
Of compost, or have inched by intervals
Through tidy gardens to this ivy bed.

And here, dim-eyed, but ears so sensitive
A voice within the house can make him freeze,
He scuffs the edge of danger, yet can live
Happily in our nights and absences.

A country creature, wary, quiet and shrewd,
He takes the milk we give him, when we're gone.
At night our slamming voices must sound crude
To one who sits and waits for silences.

ANTHONY THWAITE (1930–

AN ELEGY ON THE DEATH OF A MAD DOG

Good people all, of every sort,
   Give ear unto my song;
And if you find it wond'rous short,
   It cannot hold you long.

In Islington there was a man,
   Of whom the world might say,
That still a godly race he ran,
   Whene'er he went to pray.

A kind and gentle heart he had,
   To comfort friends and foes;
The naked every day he clad,
   When he put on his clothes.

And in that town a dog was found,
   As many dogs there be,
Both mongrel, puppy, whelp and hound,
   And curs of low degree.

This dog and man at first were friends;
   But when a pique began,
The dog, to gain some private ends,
   Went mad and bit the man.

Around from all the neighbouring streets
   The wondering neighbours ran,
And swore the dog had lost his wits,
   To bite so good a man.

The wound it seemed both sore and sad
   To every Christian eye;
And while they swore the dog was mad,
   They swore the man would die.

But soon a wonder came to light,
   That showed the rogues they lied:
The man recovered of the bite,
   The dog it was that died.

                      OLIVER GOLDSMITH
                          (1730?–1774)

EPIGRAM ENGRAVED ON THE COLLAR OF A DOG WHICH I GAVE TO HIS ROYAL HIGHNESS

I am his Highness' dog at Kew;
Pray tell me, sir, whose dog are you?

ALEXANDER POPE (1688–1744)

PRAISE OF A COLLIE

She was a small dog, neat and fluid –
Even her conversation was tiny:
She greeted you with *bow*, never *bow-wow*.

Her sons stood monumentally over her
But did what she told them. Each grew grizzled
Till it seemed he was his own mother's grandfather.

Once, gathering sheep on a showery day,
I remarked how dry she was. Pollóchan said, 'Ah,
It would take a very accurate drop to hit Lassie.'

And her tact – and tactics! When the sheep bolted
In an unforeseen direction, over the skyline
Came – who but Lassie, and not even panting.

She sailed in the dinghy like a proper sea-dog.
Where's a burn? – she's first on the other side.
She flowed through fences like a piece of black wind.

But suddenly she was old and sick and crippled . . .
I grieved for Pollóchan when he took her for a stroll
And put his gun to the back of her head.

                          NORMAN MacCAIG (1910–   )

ODE ON THE DEATH OF A FAVOURITE CAT, DROWNED IN A TUB OF GOLD FISHES

'Twas on a lofty vase's side,
Where China's gayest art had dyed
   The azure flowers that blow;
Demurest of the tabby kind,
The pensive Selima reclined,
   Gazed on the lake below.

Her conscious tail her joy declared;
The fair round face, the snowy beard,
   The velvet of her paws,
Her coat, that with the tortoise vies,
Her ears of jet and emerald eyes,
   She saw; and purred applause.

Still had she gazed; but 'midst the tide
Two angel forms were seen to glide,
   The Genii of the stream:
Their scaly armour's Tyrian hue
Thro' richest purple to the view
   Betray'd a golden gleam.

The hapless Nymph with wonder saw:
A whisker first and then a claw,
   With many an ardent wish,
She stretch'd in vain to reach the prize.
What female heart can gold despise?
   What Cat's averse to fish?

Presumptuous Maid! with looks intent
Again she stretch'd, again she bent,
   Nor knew the gulf between.
(Malignant Fate sat by, and smiled.)
The slipp'ry verge her feet beguiled,
   She tumbled headlong in.

Eight times emerging from the flood
She mew'd to every wat'ry god,
   Some speedy aid to send.
No Dolphin came, no Nereid stirr'd:
No cruel *Tom* nor *Susan* heard.
   A Fav'rite has no friend!

From hence, ye Beauties undeceiv'd,
Know, one false step is ne'er retriev'd,
   And be with caution bold.
Not all that tempts your wand'ring eyes
And heedless hearts, is lawful prize;
   Nor all that glisters, gold.

THOMAS GRAY (1716–71)

PANGUR BÁN

Written by a student of the monastery of Carinthia on a copy of St Paul's Epistles, in the eighth century.

I and Pangur Bán, my cat,
'Tis a like task we are at;
Hunting mice is his delight,
Hunting words I sit all night.

Better far than praise of men
'Tis to sit with book and pen;
Pangur bears me no ill-will,
He too plies his simple skill.

'Tis a merry thing to see
At our tasks how glad are we,
When at home we sit and find
Entertainment to our mind.

Oftentimes a mouse will stray
In the hero Pangur's way;
Oftentimes my keen thought set
Takes a meaning in its net.

'Gainst the wall he sets his eye
Full and fierce and sharp and sly;
'Gainst the wall of knowledge I
All my little wisdom try.

When a mouse darts from its den,
O how glad is Pangur then!
O what gladness do I prove
When I solve the doubts I love!

So in peace our tasks we ply,
Pangur Bán, my cat, and I;
In our arts we find our bliss,
I have mine and he has his.

Practice every day has made
Pangur perfect in his trade;
I get wisdom day and night,
Turning darkness into light.

ANONYMOUS

trans. from the Gaelic by
Robin Flower

THE CAT AND THE MOON

The cat went here and there
And the moon spun round like a top,
And the nearest kin of the moon,
The creeping cat, looked up.
Black Minnaloushe stared at the moon,
For, wander and wail as he would,
The pure cold light in the sky
Troubled his animal blood.
Minnaloushe runs in the grass
Lifting his delicate feet.
Do you dance, Minnaloushe, do you dance?
When two close kindred meet,
What better than call a dance?
Maybe the moon may learn,
Tired of that courtly fashion,
A new dance turn.

Minnaloushe creeps through the grass
From moonlit place to place,
The sacred moon overhead
Has taken a new phase.
Does Minnaloushe know that his pupils
Will pass from change to change,
And that from round to crescent,
From crescent to round they range?
Minnaloushe creeps through the grass
Alone, important and wise,
And lifts to the changing moon
His changing eyes.

W.B. YEATS (1865–1939)

THE NAMING OF CATS

The Naming of Cats is a difficult matter,
   It isn't just one of your holiday games;
You may think at first I'm as mad as a hatter
When I tell you, a cat must have THREE DIFFERENT NAMES.
First of all, there's the name that the family use daily,
   Such as Peter, Augustus, Alonzo or James,
Such as Victor or Jonathan, George or Bill Bailey –
All of them sensible everyday names.
There are fancier names if you think they sound sweeter,
   Some for the gentlemen, some for the dames:
Such as Plato, Admetus, Electra, Demeter –
But all of them sensible everyday names.
But I tell you, a cat needs a name that's particular,
   A name that's peculiar, and more dignified,
Else how can he keep up his tail perpendicular,

Or spread out his whiskers, or cherish his pride?
Of names of this kind, I can give you a quorum,
   Such as Munkustrap, Quaxo, or Coricopat,
Such as Bombalurina, or else Jellylorum –
Names that never belong to more than one cat.
But above and beyond there's still one name left over,
And that is the name that you never will guess;
The name that no human research can discover –
   But THE CAT HIMSELF KNOWS, and will never confess.
When you notice a cat in profound meditation,
   The reason, I tell you, is always the same:
His mind is engaged in a rapt contemplation
     Of the thought, of the thought, of the thought of his name:
         His ineffable effable
         Effinineffable
Deep and inscrutable singular Name.

                    T.S. ELIOT (1888–1965)

EPITAPH ON A HARE

   Here lies, whom hound did ne'er pursue,
     Nor swifter greyhound follow,
   Whose foot ne'er tainted morning dew,
     Nor ear heard huntsman's 'hollo',

   Old Tiney, surliest of his kind,
     Who, nursed with tender care,
   And to domestic bounds confined,
     Was still a wild jack-hare.

Though duly from my hand he took
    His pittance ev'ry night,
He did it with a jealous look,
    And, when he could, would bite.

His diet was of wheaten bread,
    And milk, and oats, and straw,
Thistles, or lettuces instead,
    With sand to scour his maw.

On twigs of hawthorn he regaled,
    On pippins' russet peel;
And when his juicy salads failed,
    Sliced carrot pleased him well.

A Turkey carpet was his lawn,
    Whereon he loved to bound,
To skip and gambol like a fawn,
    And swing his rump around.

His frisking was at evening hours,
    For then he lost his fear;
But most before approaching show'rs,
    Or when a storm drew near.

Eight years and five round-rolling moons
    He thus saw steal away,
Dozing out all his idle noons,
    And ev'ry night at play.

I kept him for his humour's sake,
    For he would oft beguile
My heart of thoughts that made it ache,
    And force me to a smile.

But now, beneath this walnut-shade
    He finds his long, last home,
And waits in snug concealment laid,
    Till gentler Puss shall come.

He, still more agèd, feels the shocks
    From which no care can save,
And, partner once of Tiney's box,
    Must soon partake his grave.

WILLIAM COWPER (1731–1800)

EPITAPH ON A DORMOUSE, REALLY WRITTEN BY A LITTLE BOY

In Paper Case,
Hard by this Place,
Dead a poor Dormouse lies;
And soon or late,
Summon'd by Fate,
Each Prince, each Monarch dies

Ye Sons of Verse,
While I rehearse,
Attend instructive Rhyme;
Nor Sins had *Dor*,
To answer for,
Repent of yours in Time.

ANONYMOUS

(From *The History of Little Goody Two-Shoes*, 1765)

SONNET TO A MONKEY

O lovely O most charming pug
Thy gracefull air & heavenly mug
The beauties of his mind do shine
And every bit is shaped so fine
Your very tail is most devine
Your teeth is whiter then the snow
Yor are a great buck & a bow
Your eyes are of so fine a shape
More like a christains then an ape
His cheeks is like the roses blume
Your hair is like the ravens plume
His noses cast is of the roman
He is a very pretty weomen
I could not get a rhyme for roman
And was oblidged to call it weoman.

MARJORY FLEMING (1803–11)

This is the poem exactly as Marjory wrote it when she was seven. 'Pug' was the colloquial term for a monkey.

THE FROG

Be kind and tender to the Frog,
And do not call him names,
As 'Slimy skin', or 'Polly-wog',
Or likewise 'Ugly James',

    Or 'Gap-a-grin', or 'Toad-gone wrong',
      Or 'Bill Bandy-knees':
    The Frog is justly sensitive
      To epithets like these.
    No animal will more repay
      A treatment kind and fair;
    At least so lonely people say
    Who keep a frog (and, by the way,
      They are extremely rare).

HILAIRE BELLOC (1870–1953)

THE PYTHON

A Python I should not advise
It needs a doctor for its eyes,
And has the measles yearly.
However, if you feel inclined
To get one (to improve your mind,
And not from fashion merely),
Allow no music near its cage;
And when it flies into a rage
Chastise it, most severely.
I had an aunt in Yucatan
Who bought a Python from a man
    And kept it for a pet.
She died, because she never knew
These simple little rules and few; –
The Snake is living yet.

HILAIRE BELLOC (1870–1953)

ROAD-SONG OF THE *BANDAR-LOG*

Here we go in a flung festoon,
Half-way up to the jealous moon!
Don't you envy our pranceful bands?
Don't you wish you had extra hands?
Wouldn't you like if your tails were – *so* –
Curved in the shape of a Cupid's bow?
   Now you're angry, but – never mind,
   Brother, thy tail hangs down behind!

Here we sit in a branchy row,
Thinking of beautiful things we know;
Dreaming of deeds that we mean to do,
All complete, in a minute or two –
Something noble and grand and good,
Won by merely wishing we could.
   Now we're going to – never mind,
   Brother, thy tail hangs down behind!

All the talk we ever have heard
Uttered by bat or beast or bird –
Hide or fin or scale or feather –
Jabber it quickly and all together!
Excellent! Wonderful! Once again!
Now we are talking just like men.
   Let's pretend we are . . . never mind,
   Brother, thy tail hangs down behind!
   This is the way of the Monkey-kind.

Then join our leaping lines that scumfish through the pines,
That rocket by where, light and high, the wild-grape swings.
By the rubbish in our wake, and the noble noise we make,
Be sure, be sure, we're going to do some splendid things!

                RUDYARD KIPLING (1865–1936)
                         From *The Jungle Book*

THE TYGER

Tyger! Tyger! burning bright
In the forests of the night,
What immortal hand or eye
Could frame thy fearful symmetry?

In what distant deeps or skies
Burnt the fire of thine eyes?
On what wings dare he aspire?
What the hand dare seize the fire?

And what shoulder, and what art,
Could twist the sinews of thy heart?
And, when thy heart began to beat,
What dread hand? and what dread feet?

What the hammer? what the chain?
In what furnace was thy brain?
What the anvil? what dread grasp
Dare its deadly terrors clasp?

When the stars threw down their spears,
And water'd heaven with their tears,
Did he smile his work to see?
Did he who made the Lamb make thee?

Tyger! Tyger! burning bright
In the forests of the night,
What immortal hand or eye,
Did frame thy fearful symmetry?

WILLIAM BLAKE (1757–1827)

Two Yoruba poems
ELEPHANT

Elephant who brings death.
Elephant, a spirit in the bush.
With his single hand
He can pull two palm trees to the ground.
If he had two hands
He would tear the heavens like an old rag.
The spirit who eats dog,
The spirit who eats ram,
The spirit who eats
A whole palm fruit with its thorns.
With his four mortal legs
He tramples down the grass,
Wherever he walks,
The grass is forbidden to stand up again.
An elephant is not a load for an old man –
Nor for a young man either.

KOB ANTELOPE

A creature to pet and spoil
like a child.
Smooth skinned
stepping cautiously
in the lemon grass.
Round and plump
like a newly married wife.
The neck
heavy with brass rings.
The eyes
gentle like a bird's.

The head
beautiful like carved wood.
When you suddenly escape
you spread fine dust
like a butterfly
shaking its wings.
Your neck seems long,
so very long
to the greedy hunter.

ANONYMOUS
From the Yoruba, trans. Ulli Beier

DICK TURPIN'S RIDE ON BLACK BESS

'Dick Turpin, bold Dick, hie away' was the cry
Of my pals, who were startled, you guess.
The pistols were levelled, the bullets whizzed by,
As I jumped on the back of Black Bess.

Three officers, mounted, led forward the chase,
Resolved in the capture to share;
But I smiled on their efforts, though swift was their pace,
As I urged on my bonny black mare.

Hark away, hark away! Still onward we press,
And I saw by the glimmers of morn,
Full many a mile on the back of Black Bess
That night I was gallantly borne.

Hie over, my Bet! Thy fatigue thou must bear.
Well cleared! Never falter for breath.
Hark forward, brave girl, my bonny black mare!
We are speeding for life or for death.

When the spires of York Minster now burst on my view,
And the chimes they are ringing a knell –
Halt, halt! my brave mare, they no longer pursue.
As she halted, she staggered, she fell.

Her breathings are over, all hushed to her grave,
My poor Black Bess, once my pride.
But her heart she had burst, her rider to save –
For Dick Turpin she lived and she died.

ANONYMOUS

AT GRASS

The eye can hardly pick them out
From the cold shade they shelter in,
Till wind distresses tail and mane;
Then one crops grass, and moves about
– The other seeming to look on –
And stands anonymous again.

Yet fifteen years ago, perhaps
Two dozen distances sufficed
To fable them: faint afternoons
Of Cups and Stakes and Handicaps,
Whereby their names were artificed
To inlay faded, classic Junes –

Silks at the start: against the sky
Numbers and parasols: outside,
Squadrons of empty cars, and heat,
And littered grass: then the long cry
Hanging unhushed till it subside
To stop-press columns on the street.

Do memories plague their ears like flies?
They shake their heads. Dusk brims the shadows.
Summer by summer all stole away,
The starting-gates, the crowds and cries –
All but the unmolesting meadows.
Almanacked, their names live; they
Have slipped their names, and stand at ease,
Or gallop for what must be joy,
And not a fieldglass sees them home,
Or curious stop-watch prophesies:
Only the groom, and the groom's boy,
With bridles in the evening come.

PHILIP LARKIN (1922–85)

FIRST SIGHT

Lambs that learn to walk in snow
When their bleating clouds the air
Meet a vast unwelcome, know
Nothing but a sunless glare.
Newly stumbling to and fro
All they find, outside the fold,
Is a wretched width of cold.

As they wait beside the ewe,
Her fleeces wetly caked, there lies
Hidden round them, waiting too,
Earth's immeasurable surprise.
They could not grasp it if they knew
What so soon will wake and grow
Utterly unlike the snow.

PHILIP LARKIN (1922–85)

THE DONKEY

When fishes flew and forests walked
   And figs grew upon thorn,
Some moment when the moon was blood
   Then surely I was born.

With monstrous head and sickening cry
   And ears like errant wings,
The devil's walking parody
   On all four-footed things.

The tattered outlaw of the earth,
    Of ancient crooked will;
Starve, scourge, deride me: I am dumb,
    I keep my secret still.

Fools! For I also had my hour;
    One far fierce hour and sweet:
There was a shout about my ears,
    And palms before my feet.

G.K. CHESTERTON
(1874–1936)

FRANCIS JAMMES: A PRAYER TO GO TO PARADISE WITH THE DONKEYS

When I must come to you, O my God, I pray
It be some dusty-roaded holiday,
And even as in my travels here below,
I beg to choose by what road I shall go
To Paradise, where the clear stars shine by day.
I'll take my walking-stick and go my way,
And to my friends the donkeys I shall say,
'I am Francis Jammes, and I'm going to Paradise,
For there is no hell in the land of the loving God.'
And I'll say to them: 'Come, sweet friends of the blue skies,
Poor creatures who with a flap of the ears or a nod
Of the head shake off the buffets, the bees, the flies . . .'

Let me come with these donkeys, Lord, into your land,
These beasts who bow their heads so gently, and stand
With their small feet joined together in a fashion
Utterly gentle, asking your compassion.
I shall arrive, followed by their thousands of ears,
Followed by those with baskets at their flanks,
By those who lug the carts of mountebanks
Or loads of feather-dusters and kitchen-wares,
By those with humps of battered water-cans,
By bottle-shaped she-asses who halt and stumble,
By those tricked out in little pantaloons
To cover their wet, blue galls where flies assemble
In whirling swarms, making a drunken hum.
Dear God, let it be with these donkeys that I come,
And let it be that angels lead us in peace
To leafy streams where cherries tremble in air,
Sleek as the laughing flesh of girls; and there
In that haven of souls let it be that, leaning above
Your divine waters, I shall resemble these donkeys,
Whose humble and sweet poverty will appear
Clear in the clearness of your eternal love.

RICHARD WILBUR (1921-   )

THE OX-TAMER

In a far-away northern county in the placid pastoral region,
Lives my farmer friend, the theme of my recitative, a famous tamer
                                               of oxen,
There they bring him the three-year-olds and the four-year-olds, to
                                               break them,
He will take the wildest steer in the world and break him and tame him,

He will go fearless without any whip where the young bullock
                              chafes up and down the yard,
The bullock's head tosses restless high in the air with raging eyes,
Yet see you! how soon his rage subsides – how soon this tamer
                              tames him;
See you! on the farms hereabouts a hundred oxen young and old, and
                              he is the man who has tamed them,
They all know him, all are affectionate to him;
See you! some are such beautiful animals, so lofty looking;
Some are buff-color'd, some mottled, one has a white line running
                              along his back, some are brindled,
Some have wide flaring horns (a good sign) – see you! the bright hides,
See, the two with stars on their foreheads – see, the round bodies
                              and broad backs,
How straight and square they stand on their legs – what fine
                              sagacious eyes!
How they watch their tamer – they wish him near them – how they
                              turn to look after him!
What yearning expression! how uneasy they are when he moves
                              away from them;
Now I marvel what it can be he appears to them (books, politics,
                              poems, depart – all else departs,)
I confess I envy only his fascination - my silent, illiterate friend,
Whom a hundred oxen love there in his life on farms,
In the northern county far, in the placid pastoral region.

                              WALT WHITMAN (1819–92)

THE OXEN

Christmas Eve, and twelve of the clock.
   'Now they are all on their knees,'
An elder said as we sat in a flock
   By the embers in hearthside ease.

We pictured the meek mild creatures where
   They dwelt in their strawy pen,
Nor did it occur to one of us there
   To doubt they were kneeling then.

So fair a fancy few would weave
   In these years! Yet, I feel,
If someone said on Christmas Eve,
   'Come, see the oxen kneel

'In the lonely barton by yonder coomb
   Our childhood used to know,'
I should go with him in the gloom,
   Hoping it might be so.

THOMAS HARDY (1840–1928)

CAROL OF BIRDS, BEASTS AND MEN

Christus natus est! the cock	*Christ is born*
Carols on the morning dark.	
Quando? croaks the raven stiff	*When?*
Freezing on the broken cliff.	

Hoc nocte, replies the crow　　　　　　　　　　*This night*
Beating high above the snow.

Ubi? Ubi? booms the ox　　　　　　　　　　　*Where?*
From its cavern in the rocks.

Bethlehem, then bleats the sheep
Huddled on the winter steep.

Quomodo? the brown hare clicks　　　　　　　　*How?*
Chattering among the sticks.

Humiliter, the careful wren　　　　　　　　　　*Humbly*
Thrills upon the cold hedge-stone.

Cur? Cur? sounds the coot　　　　　　　　　　*Why?*
By the iron river-root.

Propter homine, the thrush　　　　　　*For the sake of man*
Sings on the sharp holly-bush.

Cui? Cui? rings the chough　　　　　　　　　*To whom?*
On the strong, sea-haunted bluff.

Mary! Mary! calls the lamb
From the quiet of the womb.

Praeterea ex quo? cries　　　　　　　　　　　*Who else?*
The woodpecker in pallid skies.

Joseph, breathes the heavy shire
Warming in its own blood-fire.

Ultime ex quo? the owl   *Who above all?*
Solemnly begins to call.

De Deo, the little stare   *Of God*
Whistles on the hardening air.

Pridem? Pridem? the jack snipe   *Long ago?*
From the stiff grass starts to pipe.

Sic et non, answers the fox   *Yes and no*
Tiptoeing the bitter lough.

Quomodo hoc scire potest?   *How do I know this?*
Boldly flutes the robin-redbreast.

Illo in eandem, squeaks   *By going there*
The mouse within the barley-sack.

Quae sarcinae? asks the daw   *What luggage?*
Swaggering from head to claw.

Nulla res, replies the ass   *None*
Bearing on its back the cross.

Quantum pecuniae? shrills   *How much money?*
The wandering gull about the hills.

Ne nummum quidem, the rook   *Not a penny*
Caws across the rigid brook.

Nulla resne? barks the dog   *Nothing at all?*
By the crumbling fire-log.

Nil nisi cor amans, the dove   *Only a loving heart*
Murmurs from its house of love.

Gloria in Excelsis! Then
Man is God and God is Man.

                                                    CHARLES CAUSLEY (1917–   )

Childhood and youth

IT IS INDEED SPINACH

People by whom I am riled
Are people who go around wishing O that Time would backward turn backward and again make them a child.
Either they have no sense, or else they go round repeating something they have heard like a parakeet,
Or else they deliberately prevarikete.
Because into being a marathon dancer or a chiropodist or a tea-taster or a certified public accountant I would not be beguiled,
But I would sooner than I would into being again a child,
Because being a child is not much of a pastime,
And I don't want any next time because I remember the last time.
I do not wish to play with my toes,
Nor do I wish to have cod-liver oil spooned down my throat or albolene pushed up my nose.
I don't want to be plopped down at sundown into a crib or a cradle
And if I don't go to sleep right away to be greeted with either a lullaby or an upbraidal.
I can think of nothing worse
Than never being out of sight of a parent or a nurse;
Yes, that is the part that I don't see how they survive it,
To have their private life so far from private.
Furthermore, I don't want to cry for the moon,
And I do want to hold my own spoon;
I have more ambitious ideas of a lark
Than to collect pebbles in my hat or be taken for a walk in the park;
I should hate to be held together with safety pins instead of buttons and suspenders and belts,
And I should particularly hate being told every time I was doing something I liked that it was time to do something else.

So it's pooh for the people who want Time to make them a child
   again, because I think that they must already be a child again or
   else they would stand up and own up
That it's much more fun to be a grown-up.

OGDEN NASH (1902–71)

CHILDREN'S PARTY

May I join you in the doghouse, Rover?
I wish to retire till the party's over.
Since three o'clock I've done my best
To entertain each tiny guest;
My innocence now I've left behind me,
And if they want me, let them find me.
I blew their bubbles, I sailed their boats,
I kept them from each other's throats.
I told them tales of magic lands,
I took them out to wash their hands.
I sorted their rubbers and tied their laces,
I wiped their noses and dried their faces.
Of similarity there's lots
'Twixt tiny tots and Hottentots.
I've earned enough repose to heal the ravages
Of these angelic-looking savages.
Oh progeny playing by itself
Is a lonely fascinating elf.
But progeny in roistering batches
Would drive St Francis from here to Natchez.
Shunned are the games a parent proposes;
They prefer to squirt each other with hoses.

Their playmates are their natural foemen,
And they like to poke each other's abdomen.
Their joy needs another's woe to cushion it,
Say a puddle, and somebody littler to push in it.
They observe with glee the ballistic results
Of ice cream with spoons for catapults,
And inform the assembly with tears and glares,
That everybody's presents are better than theirs.
Oh little women and little men,
Someday I hope to love you again.
But not till after the party's over,
So give me the key to the doghouse, Rover.

OGDEN NASH (1902–71)

INDOOR GAMES NEAR NEWBURY

In among the silver birches winding ways of tarmac wander
And the signs to Bussock Bottom, Tussock Wood and Windy Brake,
Gabled lodges, tile-hung churches, catch the light of our Lagonda
As we drive to Wendy's party, lemon curd and Christmas cake.
   Rich the makes of motor whirring,
   Past the pine-plantation purring,
     Come up, Hupmobile, Delage!
   Short the way your chauffeurs travel,
   Crunching over private gravel,
     Each from out his warm garáge.

Oh but Wendy, when the carpet yielded to my indoor pumps
   There you stood, your gold hair streaming,
   Handsome in the hall-light gleaming,

There you looked and there you led me off into the game of clumps,
   Then the new Victrola playing
   And your funny uncle saying
'Choose your partners for a fox-trot! Dance until it's *tea* o'clock!
   'Come on, young 'uns, foot it featly!'
   Was it chance that paired us neatly,
   I, who loved you so completely,
You, who pressed me closely to you, hard against your party frock.

'Meet me when you've finished eating!' So we met and no one
                                             found us.
Oh that dark and furry cupboard while the rest played hide and seek!
Holding hands our two hearts beating in the bedroom silence
                                             round us,
Holding hands and hardly hearing sudden footsteps, thud and shriek.
   Love that lay too deep for kissing –
   'Where *is* Wendy? Wendy's missing!'
     Love so pure it *had* to end,
   Love so strong that I was frighten'd
   When you gripped my fingers tight and
Hugging, whispered 'I'm your friend.'

Good-bye Wendy! Send the fairies, pinewood elf and larch tree gnome,
   Spingle-spangle stars are peeping
   At the lush Lagonda creeping
Down the winding ways of tarmac to the leaded lights of home.
   There, among the silver birches,
   All the bells of all the churches
Sounded in the bath-waste running out into the frosty air.
   Wendy speeded my undressing,
   Wendy's in the sheet's caressing,
   Wendy bending gives a blessing,
Holds me as I drift to dreamland, safe inside my slumber-wear.

                                      SIR JOHN BETJEMAN
                                      (1906–84)

HUNTER TRIALS

It's awf'lly bad luck on Diana,
   Her ponies have swallowed their bits,
She fished down their throats with a spanner
   And frightened them all into fits.

So now she's attempting to borrow,
   Do lend her some, Mummy, *do*;
I'll lend her my own for to-morrow,
   But to-day *I'll* be wanting them too.

Just look at Prunella on Guzzle,
   The wizardest pony on earth;
Why doesn't she slacken his muzzle
   And tighten the breech in his girth?

I say, Mummy, there's Mrs Geyser
   And doesn't she look pretty sick?
I bet it's because Mona Lisa
   Was hit on the hock with a brick.

Miss Blewitt says Monica threw it,
   But Monica says it was Joan,
And Joan's very thick with Miss Blewitt,
   So Monica's sulking alone.

And Margaret failed in her paces,
   Her withers got tied in a noose,
So her coronets caught in the traces
   And now all her fetlocks are loose.

Oh, it's me now. I'm terribly nervous.
   I wonder if Smudges will shy.
She's practically certain to swerve as
   Her Pelham is over one eye.

* * *

Oh wasn't it naughty of Smudges!
Oh, Mummy, I'm sick with disgust.
She threw me in front of the Judges,
And my silly old collarbone's bust.

SIR JOHN BETJEMAN
(1906–84)

PRAISE OF A CHILD

A child is like a rare bud.
A child is precious like coral.
A child is precious like brass.
You cannot buy a child on the market.
Not for all the money in the world.
The child you can buy for money is a slave.
We may have twenty slaves,
We may have twenty labourers,
Only a child brings us joy,
One's child is one's child.
The buttocks of our child are not so flat
That we should tie the beads on another child's hips.
One's child is one's child.
It may have a watery head or a square head,
One's child is one's child.
It is better to leave behind a child,
Than to let the slaves inherit one's house.
One must not rejoice too soon over a child,
Only the one who is buried by his child,
Is the one who has truly borne a child.
On the day of our death, our hand cannot hold a single cowry,
We need a child to inherit our belongings.

ANONYMOUS
From the Yoruba, trans. Ulli Beier

TO HIS SAVIOUR, A CHILD: A PRESENT BY A CHILD

Go, pretty child, and bear this flower
Unto thy little Saviour;
And tell Him, by that bud now blown,
He is the Rose of Sharon known.
When thou hast said so, stick it there
Upon His bib or stomacher;
And tell Him, for good handsel too,
That thou hast brought a whistle new,
Made of a clean straight oaten reed,
To charm His cries at time of need.
Tell him, for coral, thou hast none,
But if thou hadst, He should have one;
But poor thou art, and known to be
Even as moneyless as He.
Lastly, if thou canst win a kiss
From those mellifluous lips of His;
Then never take a second on,
To spoil the first impression.

ROBERT HERRICK (1591–1674)

THE ECHOING GREEN

The Sun does arise,
And make happy the skies;
The merry bells ring,
To welcome the Spring;
The skylark and thrush,
The birds of the bush,

Sing louder around
To the bells' cheerful sound,
While our sports shall be seen
On the Echoing Green.

Old John, with white hair,
Does laugh away care,
Sitting under the oak,
Among the old folk.
They laugh at our play,
And soon they all say:
'Such, such were the joys,
When we all, girls and boys,
In our youth-time were seen
On the Echoing Green.'

Till the little ones, weary,
No more can be merry;
The sun does descend,
And our sports have an end.
Round the laps of their mothers
Many sisters and brothers,
Like birds in their nest,
Are ready for rest,
And sport no more seen
On the darkening Green.

WILLIAM BLAKE (1757–1827)

LAUGHING SONG

When the green woods laugh with the voice of joy,
And the dimpling stream runs laughing by;
When the air does laugh with our merry wit,
And the green hill laughs with the noise of it;

When the meadows laugh with lively green,
And the grasshopper laughs in the merry scene;
When Mary and Susan and Emily
With their sweet round mouths sing 'Ha, ha, he!'

When the painted birds laugh in the shade,
When our table with cherries and nuts is spread:
Come live, and be merry, and join with me,
To sing the sweet chorus of 'Ha, ha, he!'

WILLIAM BLAKE (1757–1827)

BABY SONG

From the private ease of Mother's womb
I fall into the lighted room.

Why don't they simply put me back
Where it is warm and wet and black?

But one thing follows on another.
Things were different inside Mother.

Padded and jolly I would ride
The perfect comfort of her inside.

They tuck me in a rustling bed
– I lie there, raging, small, and red.

I may sleep soon, I may forget,
But I won't forget that I regret.

A rain of blood poured round her womb,
But all time roars outside this room.

THOM GUNN (1929–)

YORUBA LULLABIES

Be quiet child, and do not cry
I shall bring you a big toad
From our farm in Awututu.
Be quiet child, and do not cry.

Do not cry my child,
Your mother went to the farm,
With her big breast:
Do not cry my child.
Soon she will return with her big breast.

Why should you weep, Olukorondo,
A thorn never pricks a child's foot,
Don't I carry you on my back?
Why should you weep, O Olukorondo.

Where is Taiwo?
Where is Taiwo?
Taiwo is at home;
Let him not be too hot,
Let him not be too cold,
Princely manners,
Princely manners,
Taiwo shall have.

> ANONYMOUS
> From the Yoruba, trans. Ulli Beier

LULLABY

Golden slumbers kiss your eyes,
Smiles awake you when you rise.
Sleep, pretty wantons, do not cry,
And I will sing a lullaby:
Rock them, rock them, lullaby.

Care is heavy, therefore sleep you;
You are care, and care must keep you.
Sleep, pretty wantons, do not cry,
And I will sing a lullaby:
Rock them, rock them, lullaby.

> THOMAS DEKKER
> (1570?–1641?)

COSSACK LULLABY

Now fall asleep, my lovely babe,
   Baioushki, baiou;
The moon into your cradle looks
   The clear night through.

A story I will tell you now,
   A song I'll sing for you;
So shut your eyes and fall asleep,
   Baioushki, baiou.

The foaming Terek rushes on
   His stony shores between,
And there the wicked Chechen creeps
   And whets his dagger keen.

But father is a warrior bold,
   A fighter hard and true;
So sleep, my baby, calmly sleep,
   Baioushki, baiou.

So when the time is come you'll know
   The way a man should fight,
And leap into the saddle straight
   And sling your gun aright.

And I will work your saddle-cloth
   With scarlet silk and blue;
So sleep, my dearest, fall asleep,
   Baioushki, baiou.

And you will have a Cossack's heart
   And be a champion high,
When I come out to see you go,
   And you shall wave good-bye.

How many bitter quiet tears
   I'll weep that night for you!
Sleep sweetly, quietly, my love,
   Baioushki, baiou.

For you I shall begin to long
   And comfortless to wait;
Be kneeling early at my prayers.
   And telling fortunes late.

And I shall think how, far away,
   You must be pining too;
Oh, sleep, while not a care is yours,
   Baioushki, baiou.
I'll give you for your journeyings
   An ikon blest and small;
Put it before you when you pray,
   That God may hear your call.

And always on your mother think
   When you must arm anew;
Now, fall asleep, my darling love,
   Baioushki, baiou.

                    MIKHAIL YURIEVICH
                    LERMONTOV (1814–41)

                      trans. Frances Cornford and Esther Polianowsky Salaman

TO HIS SON, VINCENT CORBET

What I shall leave thee, none can tell,
But all shall say I wish thee well:
I wish thee, Vin, before all wealth,
Both bodily and ghostly health;
Nor too much wealth, nor wit come to thee,
So much of either may undo thee.
I wish thee learning, not for show,
Enough for to instruct and know;
Not such as gentlemen require,
To prate at table or at fire.
I wish thee all thy mother's graces,
Thy father's fortunes and his places.
I wish thee friends, and one at Court,
Not to build on, but support;
To keep thee not in doing many
Oppressions, but from suffering any.
I wish thee peace in all thy ways,
Nor lazy nor contentious days;
And, when thy soul and body part,
As innocent as now thou art.

RICHARD CORBET (1582–1635)

WISHES FOR HIS DAUGHTER

I wish your lamp and vessel
 full of oil,
Like the Wise Virgins,
 (which all fools neglect),
And the rich pearl,
 for which the merchants toil,
Yea, how to purchase
 are so circumspect:
  I wish you that white stone
   with the new name,
  Which none can read
   but who possess the same.

I wish you neither poverty
 nor riches,
But godliness,
 so gainful, with content;
No painted pomp,
 nor glory that bewitches;
A blameless life
 is the best monument:
  And such a soul
   that soars above the sky,
  Well pleas'd to live
   but better pleas'd to die.

    I wish you such a heart
      as Mary had,
  Minding the main;
      open'd as Lydia's was:
A hand like Dorcas
    who the naked clad;
Feet like Joanna's,
      posting to Christ apace,
        And above all,
          to live your self to see
          Married to Him
            who must your Saviour be.

HUGH PETERS (1598–1660)

AUTOBIOGRAPHY

In my childhood trees were green
And there was plenty to be seen.
Come back early or never come.

My father made the walls resound,
He wore his collar the wrong way round.
Come back early or never come.

My mother wore a yellow dress,
Gently, gently, gentleness.
Come back early or never come.

When I was five the black dreams came;
Nothing after that was quite the same.
Come back early or never come.

The dark was talking to the dead;
The lamp was dark beside my bed.
   Come back early or never come.

When I woke they did not care,
Nobody, nobody was there.
   Come back early or never come.

When my silent terror cried
Nobody, nobody replied.
   Come back early or never come.

I got up; the chilly sun
Saw me walk away alone.
   Come back early or never come.

LOUIS MacNEICE (1907–63)

PALM LEAVES OF CHILDHOOD

When I was very small indeed,
and Joe and Fred were six-year giants,
My father, they and I, with soil
did mix farm-yard manure.
In this we planted coconuts,
naming them by brothers' names.
The palms grew faster far than I;
and soon, ere I could grow a Man,
they, flowering, reached their goal!
Like the ear-rings that my sisters wore
came the tender golden flowers.
I watched them grow from gold to green;
then nuts as large as Tata's head.

I craved the milk I knew they bore.
I listened to the whispering leaves:
to the chattering, rattling, whispering leaves,
when night winds did wake.
They haunt me still in work and play:
those whispering leaves behind the slit
on the cabin wall of childhood's
dreaming and becoming.

GEORMBEEYI
ADALI-MORTTI

ME, COLORED

Aunt Liza.
Yes?
What am I?
What are you talking about?
I met a boy at the river.
He said he was Zulu.
    She laughed.
You are Colored.
There are three kinds of people:
White people, Colored people,
And Black people.
The White people come first,
Then the Colored people,
Then the Black people.
Why?
Because it is so.

Next day when I met Joseph,
I smacked my chest and said:
   Me, Colored!
He clapped his hands and laughed.
Joseph and I spent most
Of the long summer afternoons together.
He learnt some Afrikaans from me.
I learnt some Zulu from him.
Our days were full.
There was the river to explore.
There were many swimming lessons.
I learnt to fight with sticks;
to weave a green hat
of young willow wands and leaves;
to catch frogs and tadpoles
with my hands;
to set a trap for the *springhaas*;
to make the sounds of the river birds.
There was the hot sun to comfort us.
There was the green grass to dry our bodies.
There was the soft clay with which to build.
There was the fine sand with which to fight.
There were our giant grasshoppers to race.
There were the locust swarms
when the skies turned black
and we caught them by the hundreds.
There was the rare taste of crisp,
brown-baked, salted locusts.
There was the voice of the heavens
in the thunderstorms.

There were the voices of two children
in laughter, ours.
There were Joseph's tales of black kings
who lived in days before the white man.
At home, I said:
Aunt Liza.
Yes?
Did we have Colored kings before the white man?
No.
Then where did we come from?
Joseph and his mother came from the
black kings who were before the white man.
Laughing and ruffling my head, she said:
You talk too much. Go'n wash up.

PETER ABRAHAMS (1919–   )
From *Tell Freedom*

CHILDHOOD

I used to think that grown-up people chose
To have stiff backs and wrinkles round their nose,
And veins like small fat snakes on either hand,
On purpose to be grand.
'Till through the banisters I watched one day
My great aunt Etty's friend, who was going away,
And how her onyx beads had come unstrung.
I saw her grope to find them as they rolled;
And then I knew that she was helplessly old,
As I was helplessly young.

FRANCES CORNFORD
(1886–1960)

BOY AT THE WINDOW

Seeing the snowman standing all alone
In dusk and cold is more than he can bear.
The small boy weeps to hear the wind prepare
A night of gnashings and enormous moan.
His tearful sight can hardly reach to where
The pale-faced figure with bitumen eyes
Returns him such a god-forsaken stare
As outcast Adam gave to Paradise.

The man of snow is, nonetheless, content,
Having no wish to go inside and die.
Still he is moved to see the youngster cry.
Though frozen, water is his element.
He melts enough to drop from one soft eye
A trickle of the purest rain, a tear
For the child at the bright pane, surrounded by
Such warmth, such light, such love, and so much fear.

RICHARD WILBUR (1921-)

WHITE SNOW

'White snow,' my daughter says, and sees
For the first time the lawn, the trees,
Loaded with this superfluous stuff.
Two words suffice to make facts sure
To her, whose mental furniture
Needs only words to say enough.

Perhaps by next year she'll forget
What she today saw delicate
On every blade of grass and stone,
Yet will she recognize those two
Syllables, and see them through
Eyes which remain when snow has gone?

Season by season, she will learn
The names when seeds sprout, leaves turn,
And every change is commonplace.
She will bear snowfalls in the mind,
Know wretchedness of rain and wind,
With the same eyes in a different face.

My wish for her, who held by me
Looks out now on this mystery,
Which she has solved with words of mine,
Is that she may learn to know
That in her words for the white snow
Change and permanence combine –
The snow melted, the trees green,
Sure words for hurts not suffered yet, nor seen.

ANTHONY THWAITE

(1930–)

THE GAME

'Hide' was the word, for most of us were hiders,
'And seek' began by warning with a shout.
Attics and barns and trees were best providers:
In some of them they never found us out.

Count to five hundred: Five, ten, fifteen, twen'y
(To be last one home, is half the game),
Till the slow shadows find the dwindling many
Cheating the supper bell of prior claim.

Out of our time, O strict exiguous memory,
What have we sought, and seeking, failed or found,
Which in the instrument of simple summary
Excels the love of old enchanted ground?

The ingle, nook, and hour all have vanished,
The hidden and the hider, done and by;
But in the child runs still the sweet untarnished
'You're it', 'Five hundred', 'coming, coming', I cry.

DAVID McCORD (1897-   )

THE BIRCHED SCHOOLBOY

Hey, hey, by this day,
What availeth it me though I say nay?

I would fain be a clerk,
But yet it is a strange work;
The birch twigs be so sharp
It maketh me to have a faint heart;
    What availeth it me though I say nay?

On Monday in the morning when I shall rise,
At six of the clock, it is the gise,
To go to school without avise,
I had liefer go twenty mile twice;
    What availeth it me though I say nay?

My master looketh as he were mad:
'Where hast thou been, thou sorry lad?'
'Milked ducks, my mother bade.'
It was no marvel then I was sad;
    What availeth it me though I say nay?

My master peppered my arse with well good speed;
It was worse than fennel seed;
He would not leave till it did bleed;
Much sorrow have he for his deed!
    What availeth it me though I say nay?

gise: custom; *avise*: argument; *milked duck* . . .: mind your own business

I would my master were a watt,
And my book a wild cat,
And a brace of greyhounds in his top;
I would be glad for to see that.
    What availeth it me though I say nay?

I would my master were an hare,
And all his books hounds were,
And I myself a jolly hunter:
To blow my horn I would not spare,
For if he were dead I would not care.
    What availeth it me though I say nay?

ANONYMOUS

watt: hare

THE SCHOOLBOY

I love to rise in a summer morn
When the birds sing on every tree;
The distant huntsman winds his horn,
And the sky-lark sings with me.
O! what sweet company.

But to go to school in a summer morn,
O! it drives all joy away;
Under a cruel eye outworn,
The little ones spend the day
In sighing and dismay.

Ah! then at times I drooping sit,
And spend many an anxious hour,
Nor in my book can I take delight,
Nor sit in learning's bower,
Worn thro' with the dreary shower.

How can the bird that is born for joy
Sit in a cage and sing?
How can a child, when fears annoy,
But droop his tender wing,
And forget his youthful spring?

O! father and mother, if buds are nipp'd
And blossoms blown away,
And if the tender plants are stripp'd
Of their joy in the springing day,
By sorrow and care's dismay,

How shall the summer arise in joy,
Or the summer fruits appear?
Or how shall we gather what griefs destroy,
Or bless the mellowing year,
When the blasts of winter appear?

WILLIAM BLAKE (1757–1827)

BIRCHES

When I see birches bend to left and right
Across the lines of straighter darker trees,
I like to think some boy's been swinging them.
But swinging doesn't bend them down to stay
As ice-storms do. Often you must have seen them
Loaded with ice a sunny winter morning
After a rain. They click upon themselves
As the breeze rises, and turn many-colored
As the stir cracks and crazes their enamel.
Soon the sun's warmth makes them shed crystal shells
Shattering and avalanching on the snow-crust –
Such heaps of broken glass to sweep away
You'd think the inner dome of heaven had fallen.
They are dragged to the withered bracken by the load,
And they seem not to break; though once they are bowed
So low for long, they never right themselves:
You may see their trunks arching in the woods
Years afterwards, trailing their leaves on the ground
Like girls on hands and knees that throw their hair
Before them over their heads to dry in the sun.
But I was going to say when Truth broke in
With all her matter-of-fact about the ice-storm
I should prefer to have some boy bend them
As he went out and in to fetch the cows –
Some boy too far from town to learn baseball,
Whose only play was what he found himself,
Summer or winter, and could play alone.
One by one he subdued his father's trees
By riding them down over and over again
Until he took the stiffness out of them,
And not one but hung limp, not one was left

For him to conquer. He learned all there was
To learn about not launching out too soon
And so not carrying the tree away
Clear to the ground. He always kept his poise
To the top branches, climbing carefully
With the same pains you use to fill a cup
Up to the brim, and even above the brim.
Then he flung outward, feet first, with a swish,
Kicking his way down through the air to the ground.
So was I once myself a swinger of birches.
And so I dream of going back to be.
It's when I'm weary of considerations,
And life is too much like a pathless wood
Where your face burns and tickles with the cobwebs
Broken across it, and one eye is weeping
From a twig's having lashed across it open.
I'd like to get away from earth awhile
And then come back to it and begin over.
May no fate wilfully misunderstand me
And half grant what I wish and snatch me away
Not to return. Earth's the right place for love:
I don't know where it's likely to go better.
I'd like to go by climbing a birch tree,
And climb black branches up a snow-white trunk
Toward heaven, till the tree could bear no more,
But dipped its top and set me down again.
That would be good both going and coming back.
One could do worse than be a swinger of birches.

ROBERT FROST (1874–1963)

THE BOY ACTOR

I can remember, I can remember,
The months of November and December
   Were filled for me with peculiar joys
So different from those of other boys
   For other boys would be counting the days
Until end of term and holiday times
   But I was acting in Christmas plays
While they were taken to pantomimes.
   I didn't envy their Eton suits,
Their children's dances and Christmas trees.
   My life had wonderful substitutes
For such conventional treats as these.
   I didn't envy their country larks,
Their organized games in panelled halls:
   While they made snow-men in stately parks
I was counting the curtain calls.

   I remember the auditions, the nerve-racking auditions:
Darkened auditoriums and empty, dusty stage,
Little girls in ballet dresses practising 'positions',
Gentlemen in pince-nez asking you your age.
Hopefulness and nervousness struggling within you,
Dreading that familiar phrase, 'Thank you, dear, no more.'
Straining every muscle, every tendon, every sinew
To do your dance much better than you'd ever done before.
Think of your performance. Never mind the others,
Never mind the pianist, talent must prevail.
Never mind the baleful eyes of other children's mothers
Glaring from the corners and willing you to fail.

I can remember, I can remember,
The months of November and December
   Were more significant to me
Than other months could ever be
   For they were the months of high romance
When destiny waited on tip-toe,
   When every boy actor stood a chance
Of getting into a Christmas show.
   Not for me the dubious heaven
Of being some prefect's protégé!
   Not for me the Second Eleven.
For me, two performances a day.

   Ah those first rehearsals! Only very few lines:
   Rushing home to mother, learning them by heart,
   'Enter Left, through window' – Dots to mark the cue lines:
   'Exit with the others' – still it was a part.
   Opening performance; legs a bit unsteady,
   Dedicated tension, shivers down my spine,
   Powder, grease and eye-black, sticks of make-up ready
   Leichner number three and number five and number nine.
   World of strange enchantment, magic for a small boy
   Dreaming of the future, reaching for the crown,
   Rigid in the dressing-room, listening for the call-boy
   'Overture Beginners – Everybody Down!'

I can remember, I can remember,
The months of November and December,
   Although climatically cold and damp,
Meant more to me than Aladdin's lamp,
   I see myself, having got a job,
Walking on wings along the Strand,
   Uncertain whether to laugh or sob
And clutching tightly my mother's hand,

I never cared who scored the goal
Or which side won the silver cup,
I never learnt to bat or bowl
But I heard the curtain going up.

SIR NOEL COWARD (1899–1973)

A DAUGHTER'S SONG

My father fain would have me take
   A man that hath a beard;
My mother she cries out: Alack!
   And makes me much afraid.
Forsooth! I am not old enough.
Now this is surely goodly stuff.
Faith, let my mother marry me,
Or let some young man bury me.

For I have lived these fourteen years,
   My mother knows it well.
What need she then to cast such fears,
   Can anybody tell?
As though young women do not know
That custom will not let them woo.
I would be glad if I might choose,
But I were mad if I refuse.

My mother bids me go to school,
   And learn to do some good.
'Twere well if she would let the fool
   Come home and suck a dug.
As if my father knew not yet
That maidens are for young men fit.
Give me my mind and let me wed,
Or you shall quickly find me dead.

How soon my mother hath forgot
   That ever she was young,
And how that she denied not,
   But sang another song.
I must not speak what I do think,
When I am dry I may not drink,
Though her desire be now grown old,
She must have fire when she is cold.

You see the mother loves the son,
   The father loves the maid.
What, would she have me be a nun?
   I will not be delayed.
I will not live thus idle still;
My mother shall not have her will.
My father speaketh like a man.
I will be married, do what she can.

                      ANONYMOUS

                      From Robert Jones: *The Muses Gardin for Delights*, 1610

DADDY'S HOME, SEE YOU TO-MORROW

I always found my daughters' beaux
Invisible as the emperor's clothes,
And I could hear of them no more
Than the slamming of an auto door.
My chicks would then slip up to roost;
They were, I finally deduced,
Concealing tactfully, pro tem.
Not boys from me but me from them.

                      OGDEN NASH (1902–71)

BLUE GIRLS

Twirling your blue skirts, travelling the sward
Under the towers of your seminary,
Go listen to your teachers old and contrary
Without believing a word.

Tie the white fillets then about your hair
And think no more of what will come to pass
Than bluebirds that go walking on the grass
And chattering on the air.

Practise your beauty, blue girls, before it fail;
And I will cry with my loud lips and publish
Beauty which all our power shall never establish,
It is so frail.

For I could tell you a story which is true;
I know a woman with a terrible tongue,
Blear eye fallen from blue,
All her perfections tarnished – yet it is not long
Since she was lovelier than any of you.

JOHN CROWE RANSOM
(1888–1974)

WHO?

Who is that child I see wandering, wandering
Down by the side of the quivering stream?
Why does he seem not to hear though I call to him?
Where does he come from, and what is his name?

Why do I see him at sunrise and sunset
Taking, in old-fashioned clothes, the same track?
Why, when he walks, does he cast not a shadow
Though the sun rises and falls at his back?

Why does the dust lie so thick in the hedgerow
By the great field where a horse pulls the plough?
Why do I only see meadows where houses
Stand in a line by the riverside now?

Why does he move like a wraith by the water
Soft as the thistledown on the breeze blown?
When I draw near him so that I may hear him,
Why does he say that his name is my own?

CHARLES CAUSLEY (1917–)

EPITAPH UPON A CHILD THAT DIED

Here she lies, a pretty bud,
Lately made of flesh and blood:
Who as soon fell fast asleep
As her little eyes did peep.
Give her strewings, but not stir
The earth that lightly covers her.

ROBERT HERRICK (1591–1674)

ON THE DEATH OF FRIENDS IN CHILDHOOD

We shall not ever meet them bearded in heaven,
Nor sunning themselves among the bald of hell;
If anywhere in the deserted schoolyard at twilight,
Forming a ring perhaps, or joining hands
In games whose very names we have forgotten.
Come, memory, let us seek them there in the shadows.

DONALD JUSTICE (1925-)

Some people

THE SEVEN AGES OF MAN

All the world's a stage,
And all the men and women merely players:
They have their exits and their entrances;
And one man in his time plays many parts,
His acts being seven ages. At first the infant,
Mewling and puking in the nurse's arms.
And then the whining school-boy, with his satchel
And shining morning face, creeping like snail
Unwillingly to school. And then the lover,
Sighing like furnace, with a woeful ballad
Made to his mistress' eyebrow. Then a soldier,
Full of strange oaths, and bearded like the pard,
Jealous in honour, sudden and quick in quarrel,
Seeking the bubble reputation
Even in the cannon's mouth. And then the justice,
In fair round belly with good capon lin'd,
With eyes severe, and beard of formal cut,
Full of wise saws and modern instances;
And so he plays his part. The sixth age shifts
Into the lean and slipper'd pantaloon,
With spectacles on nose and pouch on side,
His youthful hose, well sav'd, a world too wide
For his shrunk shank; and his big manly voice,
Turning again toward childish treble, pipes
And whistles in his sound. Last scene of all,
That ends this strange eventful history,
Is second childishness and mere oblivion,
Sans teeth, sans eyes, sans taste, sans everything.

WILLIAM SHAKESPEARE
(1564–1616)
As You Like It, II vii

THE BONNIE EARL OF MORAY

Ye Hielands and ye Lawlands,
    Oh! where have ye been?
They hae slain the Earl of Moray,
    And hae laid him on the green!

Oh wae betide ye, Huntly,
    And wherefore did ye sae?
I bade ye bring him wi' ye,
    But forbade ye him to slay.

He was a braw gallant,
    And he rade at the ring;
And the bonnie Earl of Moray,
    Oh! he might hae been a king.

He was a braw gallant,
    And he play'd at the ba';
And the bonnie Earl of Moray
    Was the flower amang them a'.

He was a braw gallant,
    And he play'd at the glove;
And the bonnie Earl of Moray,
    Oh! he was the Queen's luve.

Oh! lang will his lady
    Look owre the castle Doune,
Ere she sees the Earl of Moray
    Come sounding thro' the toun.

                    ANONYMOUS

THE LOOKING-GLASS

Queen Bess was Harry's daughter!

The Queen was in her chamber, and she was middling old,
Her petticoat was satin and her stomacher was gold.
Backwards and forwards and sideways did she pass,
Making up her mind to face the cruel looking-glass.
    The cruel looking-glass that will never show a lass
    As comely or as kindly or as young as once she was!

The Queen was in her chamber, a-combing of her hair,
There came Queen Mary's spirit and it stood behind her chair,
Singing, 'Backwards and forwards and sideways may you pass,
But I will stand behind you till you face the looking-glass.
    The cruel looking-glass that will never show a lass
    As lovely or unlucky or as lonely as I was!'

The Queen was in her chamber, a-weeping very sore,
There came Lord Leicester's spirit and it scratched upon the door,
Singing, 'Backwards and forwards and sideways may you pass,
But I will walk beside you till you face the looking-glass.
    The cruel looking-glass that will never show a lass
    As harsh and unforgiving or as wicked as you was!'

The Queen was in her chamber; her sins were on her head;
She looked the spirits up and down and statelily she said:
'Backwards and forwards and sideways though I've been,
Yet I am Harry's daughter and I am England's Queen!'
    And she faced the looking-glass (and whatever else there was),
    And she saw her day was over and she saw her beauty pass
    In the cruel looking-glass that can always hurt a lass
    More hard than any ghost there is or any man there was!

RUDYARD KIPLING
(1865–1936)

EPITAPH ON SALATHIEL PAVY
A CHILD OF QUEEN ELIZABETH'S CHAPEL

Weep with me, all you that read
    This little story;
And know, for whom a tear you shed
    Death's self is sorry.
'Twas a child that so did thrive
    In grace and feature,
As Heaven and Nature seem'd to strive
    Which own'd the creature.
Years he number'd scarce thirteen
    When Fates turn'd cruel,
Yet three fill'd zodiacs had he been
    The Stage's jewel;
And did act (what now we moan)
    Old men so duly,
As sooth the Parcae thought him one,
    He play'd so truly.
So, by error, to his fate
    They all consented;
But, viewing him since, alas, too late!
    They have repented;
And have sought, to give new birth,
    In baths to steep him;
But, being so much too good for earth,
    Heaven vows to keep him.

BEN JONSON (1572/3–1637)

Parcae: the Fates

THE BLIND BOY

O say, what is that thing called light,
   Which I can ne'er enjoy?
What is the blessing of the sight?
   O tell your poor blind boy!

You talk of wond'rous things you see,
   You say the sun shines bright!
I feel him warm, but how can he
   Then make it day or night?

My day or night myself I make,
   Whene'er I wake or play;
And could I ever keep awake,
   It would be always day.

With heavy sighs I often hear
   You mourn my hopeless woe;
But sure with patience I may bear
   A loss I ne'er can know.

Then let not what I cannot have
   My cheer of mind destroy.
Thus while I sing, I am a king,
   Although a poor blind boy!

                COLLEY CIBBER (1671–1757)

THE LITTLE PLOUGH-BOY

A flaxen-headed cow-boy, as simple as may be,
And next a merry plough-boy, I whistled o'er the lea;
But now a saucy footman, I strut in worsted lace,
And soon I'll be a butler, and wag my jolly face;
When steward I'm promoted, I'll snip a tradesman's bill,
My master's coffers empty, my pockets for to fill;
When lolling in my chariot, so great a man I'll be,
You'll forget the little plough-boy that whistled o'er the lea.

I'll buy votes at elections, but when I've made the pelf,
I'll stand poll for the Parliament, and then vote in myself;
Whatever's good for me, sir, I never will oppose:
When all my Ayes are sold off, why, then I'll sell my Noes.
I'll bawl, harangue and paragraph, with speeches charm the ear,
And when I'm tired on my legs, then I'll sit down a peer.
In court or city honour, so great a man I'll be,
You'll forget the little plough-boy that whistled o'er the lea.

JOHN O'KEEFFE (1747–1833)

THE VILLAGE SCHOOLMASTER

Beside yon straggling fence that skirts the way,
With blossomed furze unprofitably gay,
There, in his noisy mansion, skilled to rule,
The village master taught his little school;
A man severe he was, and stern to view,
I knew him well, and every truant knew;
Well had the boding tremblers learned to trace
The day's disasters in his morning face;
Full well they laughed, with counterfeited glee,
At all his jokes, for many a joke had he:
Full well the busy whisper, circling round,
Conveyed the dismal tidings when he frowned;
Yet he was kind, or, if severe in aught,
The love he bore to learning was in fault;
The village all declared how much he knew;
'Twas certain he could write, and cipher too;
Lands he could measure, terms and tides presage,
And even the story ran that he could gauge.
In arguing, too, the parson owned his skill,
For, even though vanquished, he could argue still;
While words of learnèd length and thundering sound
Amazed the gazing rustics ranged around;
And still they gazed, and still the wonder grew
That one small head could carry all he knew.

OLIVER GOLDSMITH
(1730?–1774)
From *The Deserted Village*

THE SOLITARY REAPER

Behold her, single in the field,
   Yon solitary Highland Lass!
Reaping and singing by herself;
   Stop here, or gently pass!
Alone she cuts and binds the grain,
And sings a melancholy strain;
O listen! for the Vale profound
Is overflowing with the sound.

No Nightingale did ever chaunt
   More welcome notes to weary bands
Of travellers in some shady haunt,
   Among Arabian sands:
A voice so thrilling ne'er was heard
In spring-time from the Cuckoo-bird,
Breaking the silence of the seas
Among the farthest Hebrides.

Will no one tell me what she sings? –
   Perhaps the plaintive numbers flow
For old, unhappy, far-off things,
   And battles long ago:
Or is it some more humble lay,
Familiar matter of to-day?
Some natural sorrow, loss, or pain,
That has been, and may be again?

Whate'er the theme, the Maiden sang
   As if her song could have no ending;
I saw her singing at her work,
   And o'er the sickle bending; –

I listen'd, motionless and still;
And, as I mounted up the hill,
The music in my heart I bore,
Long after it was heard no more.

WILLIAM WORDSWORTH
(1770–1850)

NEGRO

I am a Negro:
    Black as the night is black,
    Black like the depths of my Africa.

I've been a slave:
    Caesar told me to keep his door-steps clean.
    I brushed the boots of Washington.

I've been a worker:
    Under my hands the pyramids arose.
    I made mortar for the Woolworth Building.

I've been a singer:
    All the way from Africa to Georgia
    I carried my sorrow songs.
    I made ragtime.

I've been a victim:
    The Belgians cut off my hands in the Congo.
    They lynch me still in Mississippi.

I am a Negro:
> Black as the night is black.
> Black like the depths of my Africa.

>> LANGSTON HUGHES
>> (1902–67)

AN OLD WOMAN OF THE ROADS

O, to have a little house!
> To own the hearth and stool and all!
The heap'd-up sods upon the fire,
> The pile of turf against the wall!

To have a clock with weights and chains
> And pendulum swinging up and down!
A dresser filled with shining delph,
> Speckled with white and blue and brown!

I could be busy all the day
> Cleaning and sweeping hearth and floor;
And fixing on their shelf again
> My white and blue and speckled store!

I could be quiet there at night
> Beside the fire and by myself,
Sure of a bed and loth to leave
> The ticking clock and the shining delph!

Och! but I'm weary of mist and dark,
> And roads where there's never a house or bush,
And tired I am of bog and road
> And the crying wind and the lonesome hush!

And I am praying to God on high,
    And I am praying Him night and day,
For a little house – a house of my own –
    Out of the wind's and the rain's way.

                  PADRAIC COLUM (1881–1972)

AUNT SUE'S STORIES

Aunt Sue has a head full of stories.
Aunt Sue has a whole heart full of stories.
Summer nights on the front porch
Aunt Sue cuddles a brown-faced child to her bosom
And tells him stories.

Black slaves
Working in the hot sun,
And black slaves
Walking in the dewy night,
And black slaves singing sorrow songs on the banks of a mighty river
Mingle themselves softly
In the flow of old Aunt Sue's voice,
Mingle themselves softly
In the dark shadows that cross and recross
Aunt Sue's stories.

And the dark-faced child, listening,
Knows that Aunt Sue never got her stories
Out of any book at all,
But that they came
Right out of her own life.

The dark-faced child is quiet
        Of a summer night
        Listening to Aunt Sue's stories.

                      LANGSTON HUGHES
                      (1902–67)

THE BALLAD OF RUDOLPH REED

Rudolph Reed was oaken.
His wife was oaken too.
And his two good girls and his good little man
Oakened as they grew.

'I am not hungry for berries.
I am not hungry for bread.
But hungry hungry for a house
Where at night a man in bed

'May never hear the plaster
Stir as if in pain.
May never hear the roaches
Falling like fat rain.

'Where never wife and children need
Go blinking through the gloom.
Where every room of many rooms
Will be full of room.

'Oh my home may have its east or west
Or north or south behind it.
All I know is I shall know it,
And fight for it when I find it.'

It was in a street of bitter white
That he made his application,
For Rudolph Reed was oakener
Than others in the nation.

The agent's steep and steady stare
Corroded to a grin.
Why, you black old, tough old hell of a man,
Move your family in!

Nary a grin grinned Rudolph Reed,
Nary a curse cursed he,
But moved in his House. With his dark little wife,
And his dark little children three.

A neighbor would *look*, with a yawning eye
That squeezed into a slit.
But the Rudolph Reeds and the children three
Were too joyous to notice it.

For were they not firm in a home of their own
With windows everywhere
And a beautiful banistered stair
And a front yard for flowers and a back yard for grass?

The first night, a rock, big as two fists.
The second, a rock big as three.
But nary a curse cursed Rudolph Reed.
(Though oaken as man could be.)

The third night, a silvery ring of glass.
Patience ached to endure.
But he looked, and lo! small Mabel's blood
Was staining her gaze so pure.

Then up did rise our Rudolph Reed
And pressed the hand of his wife,
And went to the door with a thirty-four
And a beastly butcher knife.

He ran like a mad thing into the night,
And the words in his mouth were stinking.
By the time he had hurt his first white man
He was no longer thinking.

By the time he had hurt his fourth white man
Rudolph Reed was dead.
His neighbors gathered and kicked his corpse.
'Nigger' – his neighbors said.

Small Mabel whimpered all night long.
For calling herself the cause.
Her oak-eyed mother did no thing
But change the bloody gauze.

GWENDOLYN BROOKS (1917–

SELF-PORTRAIT OF EDWARD LEAR

How pleasant to know Mr Lear!
　Who has written such volumes of stuff!
Some think him ill-tempered and queer,
　But a few think him pleasant enough.

His mind is concrete and fastidious,
　His nose is remarkably big;
His visage is more or less hideous,

    His beard it resembles a wig.
He has ears, and two eyes, and ten fingers,
    Leastways if you reckon two thumbs;
Long ago he was one of the singers,
    But now he is one of the dumbs.

He sits in a beautiful parlour,
    With hundreds of books on the wall;
He drinks a great deal of marsala,
    But never gets tipsy at all.

He has many friends, laymen and clerical;
    Old Foss is the name of his cat;
His body is perfectly spherical,
    He weareth a runcible hat.

When he walks in a waterproof white,
    The children run after him so!
Calling out, 'He's come out in his night-
    Gown, that crazy old Englishman, oh!'

He weeps by the side of the ocean,
    He weeps at the top of the hill;
He purchases pancakes and lotion,
    And chocolate shrimps from the mill.

He reads but he cannot speak Spanish,
    He cannot abide ginger-beer:
Ere the days of his pilgrimage vanish,
    How pleasant to know Mr Lear!

EDWARD LEAR (1812–88)

EDWARD LEAR

Left by his friends to breakfast alone on the white
Italian shore, his Terrible Demon arose
Over his shoulder: he wept to himself in the night,
A dirty landscape-painter who hated his nose.

The legions of cruel inquisitive They
Were so many and big like dogs; he was upset
By Germans and boats; affection was miles away:
But guided by tears he successfully reached his Regret.

How prodigious the welcome was. Flowers took his hat
And bore him off to introduce him to the tongs;
The demon's false nose made the table laugh; a cat
Soon had him waltzing madly, let him squeeze her hand;
Words pushed him to the piano to sing comic songs;

And children swarmed to him like settlers. He became a land.

W.H. AUDEN (1907–73)

A VICTORIAN ALBUM

Matriarch, admiral, pert-faced boy,
chlorotic virgin, plethoric bon-vivant,
London dandy, High Church dean or don, two
reposeful sisters (white skins never shown
to the sun, white hands that need never work).

Braid and brocade and broadcloth, made to last;
shrill watered-silk over stiff corsetry;
frock-coats, crinolines, aiglets, galloons, and lace;
costly simplicity; upright backs
against straight-backed chairs; a sword, a Bible, a fan.

Characters! Each (against tasselled drapes,
plaster balusters, pedestals) looked at the lens
with that look on which no sun could ever set,
with a poise derived from pride of birth,
race, class, property, privilege, place.

White, Protestant, English or Scotch,
all these were WE, the rest of the world being THEY –
the low-born or ill-bred, the new rich, the always-
with-us poor; heathens, and foreigners who
from Dover, when clear, could almost be seen to begin.

Turn the pages, with your anti-imperial hand.
Who has got among us now? Who on earth
is this? A mahogany-skinned and proud
young Muslim, smiling, handsome, assured.
Thanks to him, I can show him to you today.

That's Osman, who in the Mutiny saved
my grandfather's life, I suppose because
he thought it worth saving. There he stands
great among grandparents, grand among great-
uncles and aunts, he who put friendship first.

WILLIAM PLOMER (1903–73)

PETER GOOLE
WHO RUINED HIS FATHER
AND MOTHER BY EXTRAVAGANCE

Young Peter Goole, a child of nine
Gave little reason to complain.
Though an imaginative youth
He very often told the truth,
And never tried to black the eyes
Of Comrades of superior size.
He did his lessons (more or less)
Without extravagant distress,
And showed sufficient intellect,
But failed in one severe defect;
It seems he wholly lacked a sense
Of limiting the day's expense,
And money ran between his hands
Like water through the Ocean Sands.
Such conduct could not but affect
His parent's fortune, which was wrecked
Like many and many another one
By folly in a spendthrift son:
By that most tragical mischance,
An Only Child's Extravagance.

There came a day when Mr Goole
– The Father of this little fool –
With nothing in the bank at all
Was up against it, like a wall.
He wrang his hands, exclaiming, 'If
I only had a bit of Stiff
How different would be my life!'
Whereat his true and noble wife
Replied, to comfort him, 'Alas!
I said that this would come to pass!
Nothing can keep us off the rocks
But Peter's little Money Box.'
The Father, therefore (and his wife),
They prised it open with a knife –
But nothing could be found therein
Save two bone buttons and a pin.

Part II

They had to sell the house and grounds
For less than twenty thousand pounds,
And so retired, with broken hearts,
To vegetate in foreign parts,
And ended their declining years
At Blidah – which is near Algiers.
There in the course of time they died,
And there lie buried side by side.
While when we turn to Peter, he
The cause of this catastrophe,
There fell upon him such a fate
As makes me shudder to relate.
Just in its fifth and final year,
His University Career
Was blasted by the new and dread
Necessity of earning bread.

He was compelled to join a firm
Of Brokers – in the summer term!
And even now, at twenty-five,
He has to WORK to keep alive!
Yes! all day long from 10 till 4!
For half the year or even more;
With but an hour or two to spend
At luncheon with a city friend.

HILAIRE BELLOC (1870–1953)

SIR SMASHAM UPPE

Good afternoon, Sir Smasham Uppe!
We're having tea: do take a cup!
Sugar and milk? Now let me see –
Two lumps, I think? . . . Good gracious me!
The silly thing slipped off your knee!
Pray don't apologize, old chap:
A very trivial mishap!
So clumsy of you? How absurd!
My dear Sir Smasham, not a word!
Now do sit down and have another,
And tell us all about your brother –
You know, the one who broke his head.
Is the poor fellow still in bed? –
A chair –, allow me, sir! . . . Great Scott!
That was a nasty smash! Eh, what?
Oh, not at all: the chair was old –
Queen Anne, or so we have been told.
We've got at least a dozen more:
Just leave the pieces on the floor.

I want you to admire our view:
Come nearer to the window, do:
And look how beautiful . . . Tut, tut!
You didn't see that it was shut?
I hope you are not badly cut!
Not hurt? A fortunate escape!
Amazing! Not a single scrape?
And now, if you have finished tea,
I fancy you might like to see
A little thing or two I've got.
That china plate? Yes, worth a lot:
A beauty too . . . Ah, there it goes!
I trust it didn't hurt your toes?
Your elbow brushed it off the shelf?
Of course: I've done the same myself.
And now my dear Sir Smasham – Oh,
You surely don't intend to go?
You must be off? Well, come again.
So glad you're fond of porcelain!

                          E.V. RIEU (1887–1972)

EPIGRAM ON A SINGER

Swans sing before they die – 'twere no bad thing
Did certain persons die before they sing.

                          SAMUEL TAYLOR
                          COLERIDGE (1772–1834)

POST-BORE TRIOLET

    Escaped like a swallow
      I'll skim to the skies
    No more need I follow
    (Escaped like a swallow)
    Your heavy but hollow
      Unending replies
    Escaped like a swallow
      I'll skim to the skies.

FRANCES CORNFORD (1886–1

WISHES OF AN ELDERLY MAN

I wish I loved the Human Race;
I wish I loved its silly face;
I wish I liked the way it walks;
I wish I liked the way it talks;
And when I'm introduced to one
I wish I thought WHAT JOLLY FUN!

SIR WALTER A. RALEIGH
(1861–1922)

IMPROMPTU ON CHARLES II

God bless our good and gracious King,
    Whose promise none relies on,
Who never said a foolish thing,
    Nor ever did a wise one.

JOHN WILMOT,
EARL OF ROCHESTER (1647–8

THE GEORGES

George the First was always reckoned
Vile, but viler George the Second;
And what mortal ever heard
Any good of George the Third?
When from earth the Fourth descended
(God be praised!) the Georges ended.

WALTER SAVAGE
LANDOR (1775–1864)

LINES TO THE HEAD OF HIS COLLEGE

I do not love you, Dr Fell,
But why I cannot tell;
But this I know full well,
I do not love you, Dr Fell.

THOMAS BROWN (1663–1704)

FOLLOWER

My father worked with a horse-plough,
His shoulders globed like a full sail strung
Between the shafts and the furrow.
The horses strained at his clicking tongue.

An expert. He would set the wing
And fit the bright steel-pointed sock.
The sod rolled over without breaking.
At the headrig, with a single pluck

Of reins, the sweating team turned round
And back into the land. His eye
Narrowed and angled at the ground,
Mapping the furrow exactly.

I stumbled in his hob-nailed wake,
Fell sometimes on the polished sod;
Sometimes he rode me on his back
Dipping and rising to his plod.

I wanted to grow up and plough,
To close one eye, stiffen my arm.
All I ever did was follow
In his broad shadow round the farm.

I was a nuisance, tripping, falling,
Yapping always. But today
It is my father who keeps stumbling
Behind me, and will not go away.

SEAMUS HEANEY (1939–   )

Love and lovers' tales

BRIDAL MORNING

The maidens came
When I was in my mother's bower;
   I had all that I would.
     The bailey beareth the bell away
     The lily, the rose, the rose I lay.

The silver is white, red is the gold;
The robes they lay in fold.
     The bailey beareth the lull away;
     The lily, the rose, the rose I lay.

And thro the glass window shines the sun.
How should I love, and I so young?
     The bailey beareth the lull away.
     The lily, the rose, the rose I lay.

                        ANONYMOUS
                        15th–16th century

WESTERN WIND

  Western wind, when will you blow
    The small rain down can rain?
  Christ, if my love were in my arms
    And I in my bed again!

                        ANONYMOUS
                        16th century

DOWN FROM THE BRANCHES

Down from the branches fall the leaves,
A wanness comes on all the trees,
   The summer's done;
And into his last house in heaven
   Now goes the sun.

Sharp frost destroys the tender sprays,
Birds are a-cold in these short days.
   The nightingale
Is grieving that the fire of heaven
   Is now grown pale.

The swollen river rushes on
Past meadows whence the green has gone,
   The golden sun
Has fled our world. Snow falls by day,
   The nights are dumb.

About me all the world is stark,
And I am burning; in my heart
   There is a fire,
A living flame in me, the maid
   Of my desire.

Her kisses, fuel of my fire,
Her tender touches, flaming higher,
   The light of light
Dwells in her eyes; divinity
   Is in her sight.

Greek fire can be extinguished
By bitter wine; my fire is fed
   On other meat.
Yes, even the bitterness of love
   Is bitter-sweet.

                        ANONYMOUS
                        From a 13th century MS, trans. from
                        the Latin by Helen Waddell

I KNOW WHERE I'M GOING

I know where I'm going,
And I know who's going with me.
I know who I love,
But the dear knows who I'll marry.

I'll have stockings of silk,
Shoes of fine green leather,
Combs to buckle my hair
And a ring for every finger.

Feather beds are soft,
Painted rooms are bonny:
But I'd leave them all
To go with my Johnny.

Some say he's dark,
But I say he's bonny,
He's the flower of them all,
My handsome, winsome Johnny.

I know where I'm going,
And I know who's going with me.
I know who I love,
But the dear knows who I'll marry.

ANONYMOUS
Irish ballad

THE WATER IS WIDE

The water is wide, I cannot get through,
And neither have I wings to fly.
Give me a boat that will carry two,
And both shall row, my love and I.

Down in the meadows the other day,
A-gathering flowers both fine and gay,
A-gathering flowers both red and blue
I little thought what love can do.

I leaned my back up against some oak,
Thinking that he was a trusty tree,
But first he bended and then he broke,
And so did my false love to me.

I put my hand into the bush,
Thinking the fairest flower to find,
I pricked my finger to the bone,
But, oh, I left the rose behind.

A ship there is and she sails the sea,
She's loaded deep as deep can be;
But not so deep as the love I'm in,
I know not if I sink or swim.

Love is handsome and love is kind,
And love's a jewel when she is new.
But when it is old, it groweth cold,
And fades away like the morning dew.

>ANONYMOUS
>
>Somerset folk song

THE CAMBRIC SHIRT

Can you make me a cambric shirt,
   Parsley, sage, rosemary and thyme,
Without any seam or needle work?
   And you shall be a true lover of mine.

Can you wash it in yonder well,
   Parsley, sage, rosemary and thyme,
Where never sprung water, nor rain ever fell?
   And you shall be a true lover of mine.

Can you dry it on yonder thorn,
   Parsley, sage, rosemary and thyme,
Which never bore blossom since Adam was born?
   And you shall be a true lover of mine.

Now you have ask'd me questions three,
   Parsley, sage, rosemary and thyme,
I hope you'll answer as many for me,
   And you shall be a true lover of mine.

Can you find me an acre of land,
   Parsley, sage, rosemary and thyme,
Between the salt water and sea sand?
   And you shall be a true lover of mine.

Can you plow it with a ram's horn,
   Parsley, sage, rosemary and thyme,
And sow it all over with one pepper corn?
   And you shall be a true lover of mine.

Can you reap it with a sickle of leather,
   Parsley, sage, rosemary and thyme,
And bind it up with a peacock's feather?
   And you shall be a true lover of mine.

When you have done and finish'd your work,
   Parsley, sage, rosemary and thyme,
Then come to me for your cambric shirt,
   And you shall be a true lover of mine.

ANONYMOUS

SALLY IN OUR ALLEY

Of all the girls that are so smart
   There's none like pretty Sally;
She is the darling of my heart,
   And she lives in our alley.
There is no lady in the land
   Is half so sweet as Sally;
She is the darling of my heart,
   And she lives in our alley.

Her father he makes cabbage-nets,
   And through the streets does cry 'em;
Her mother she sells laces long
   To such as please to buy 'em;
But sure such folks could ne'er beget
   So sweet a girl as Sally!
She is the darling of my heart,
   And she lives in our alley.

When she is by, I leave my work
   (I love her so sincerely);
My master comes like any Turk
   And bangs me most severely;
But let him bang his bellyfull,
   I'll bear it all for Sally;
She is the darling of my heart,
   And she lives in our alley.

Of all the days that's in the week
   I dearly love but one day,
And that's the day that comes betwixt
   A Saturday and Monday;
For then I'm dressed all in my best
   To walk abroad with Sally;
She is the darling of my heart,
   And she lives in our alley.

My master carries me to church,
   And often am I blamed
Because I leave him in the lurch
   As soon as text is named;

I leave the church in sermon-time
   And slink away to Sally;
She is the darling of my heart,
   And she lives in our alley.

When Christmas comes about again,
   O, then I shall have money;
I'll hoard it up, and box it all,
   I'll give it to my honey;
And would it were ten thousand pounds,
   I'd give it all to Sally;
She is the darling of my heart,
   And she lives in our alley.

My master and the neighbours all
   Make game of me and Sally;
And, but for her, I'd better be
   A slave and row a galley;
But when my seven long years are out,
   O, then I'll marry Sally!
O, then we'll wed, and then we'll bed,
   But not in our alley.

HENRY CAREY (d. 1743)

ROMANCE

I will make you brooches and toys for your delight
Of bird-song at morning and star-shine at night.
I will make a palace fit for you and me,
Of green days in forests and blue days at sea.

I will make my kitchen, and you shall keep your room,
Where white flows the river and bright blows the broom,
And you shall wash your linen and keep your body white
In rainfall at morning and dewfall at night.

And this shall be for music, when no one else is near,
The fine song for singing, the rare song to hear!
That only I remember, that only you admire,
Of the broad road that stretches and the roadside fire.

ROBERT LOUIS
STEVENSON (1850–94)

THE CROSSED APPLE

I've come to give you fruit from out my orchard,
Of wide report.
I have trees there that bear me many apples
Of every sort.

Clear, streakèd; red and russet; green and golden;
Sour and sweet.
This apple's from a tree yet unbeholden,
Where two kinds meet, –

So that this side is red without a dapple,
And this side's hue
Is clear and snowy. It's a lovely apple.
It is for you.

Within are five black pips as big as peas,
As you will find,
Potent to breed you five great apple trees
Of varying kind.

To breed you wood for fire, leaves for shade,
Apples for sauce.
Oh, this is a good apple for a maid,
It is a cross.

Fine on the finer, so the flesh is tight,
And grained like silk.
Sweet Burning gave the red side, and the white
Is Meadow Milk.

Eat it; and you will taste more than the fruit:
The blossom, too,
The sun, the air, the darkness at the root,
The rain, the dew,

The earth we came to, and the time we flee,
The fire and the breast.
I claim the white part, maiden, that's for me.
You take the rest.

LOUISE BOGAN (1897–1970)

TO ME, FAIR FRIEND, YOU NEVER CAN BE OLD

To me, fair friend, you never can be old,
For as you were when first your eye I ey'd,
Such seems your beauty still. Three winters cold
Have from the forests shook three summers' pride,
Three beauteous springs to yellow autumn turn'd
In process of the seasons have I seen,
Three April perfumes in three hot Junes burn'd,
Since first I saw you fresh, which yet are green.
Ah! yet doth beauty, like a dial-hand,
Steal from his figure, and no pace perceiv'd;
So your sweet hue, which methinks still doth stand,
Hath motion, and mine eye may be deceiv'd:
   For fear of which, hear this, thou age unbred:
   Ere you were born was beauty's summer dead.

WILLIAM SHAKESPEARE
(1564–1616)

MY TRUE LOVE HATH MY HEART

My true Love hath my heart, and I have his,
By just exchange one for another given:
I hold his dear, and mine he cannot miss:
There never was a better bargain driven.

His heart in me, keeps me and him in one,
My heart in him, his thoughts and senses guides:
He loves my heart, for once it was his own:
I cherish his because in me it bides.

His heart, his wound, receivèd from my sight:
My heart was wounded, with his wounded heart,
For as from me, on him his hurt did light,
So still me thought in me his hurt did smart,
  Both equal hurt, in this change sought our bliss:
  My true Love hath my heart, and I have his.

SIR PHILIP SIDNEY (1554–86)

HYND HORN

'Hynd Horn fair, and Hynd Horn free,
Where was you born and what counterie?'
'In good greenwood where I was born,
But my friends they hae left me a' forlorn.

'I gave my love a gay gold wand,
It was to rule o'er fair Scotland;
And she gave me a gay gold ring,
To me it had virtue above all thing.

As long as that ring does keep its hue,
Unto you I will prove true;
But when that ring grows pale and wan,
You'll know that I love some other man.'

So he hoised his sail and away went he,
Away, away to some counterie;
But when he looked into his ring
He knew that she loved some other man.

  hynd: lad; *free*: noble; *hoised*: hoisted

So he hoised his sail and home came he,
Home, home again to his ain counterie;
The first he met upon dry land
It was an auld, auld beggar man.

'What news, what news, ye auld beggar man.
What news, what news hae ye to gie?'
'Nae news, nae news hae I to gie,
But the morn is our queen's wedding day.'

'Oh you'll gie me your begging weed
And I'll gie you my riding steed.'
'It's my begging weed's nae fit for you,
And your riding steed's too high for me.'

But be it right or be it wrong,
The begging weed he has put on:
'Now since I've got the begging weed,
Pray tell to me the begging lead.'

'Oh, you'll gang up to the heid o' yon hill,
And blaw your trumpet loud and shrill;
And you'll gang crawlin' down yon brae,
As if you could neither step nor stray.

'You'll seek frae Peter, and you'll seek frae Paul,
You'll seek frae the high to the low o' them all;
But frae nane o' them tak' ye nae thing,
Unless it comes frae the bride's ain han'.'

weed: clothes; *lead*: way of speaking; *seek*: beg

So he socht frae Peter, and he socht frae Paul,
He socht frae the high to the low o' them all,
But frae nane o' them wad he hae nae thing
Unless it came frae the bride's ain han'.

So the bride came tripping down the stair
With combs of yellow gold in her hair,
With a glass o' red wine in her han'
To gie to the auld beggar man.

Out o' the glass he drank the wine,
And into it he dropped the ring:
'Oh got you it by sea or got you it by lan',
Or got you it off o' droont man's han'?'

'I got it nae by sea nor yet by lan',
Nor yet did I on a droont man's han';
But I got it frae you in my wooin' gay,
And I'll gie't to you on your wedding day.'

She tore the gold down frae her heid,
'I'll follow you and beg my breid',
She tore the gold down frae her hair,
Says, 'I'll follow you for evermair.'

So atween the kitchen and the ha'
And there he let his duddy cloak fa';
He shone wi' gold aboon them a',
And the bride frae the bridegroom's stown awa'.

ANONYMOUS

droont: drowned; *duddy*: ragged; *stown*: stolen

THE GAY GOSHAWK

'O well is me, my gay goshawk,
    That you can speak and flee;
For you can carry a love-letter
    To my true Love from me.'

'O how can I carry a letter to her?
    Or how should I her know?
I bear a tongue ne'er with her spake,
And eyes that ne'er her saw.'

'O well shall ye my true Love ken
    So soon as ye her see:
For of all the flowers of fair England,
    The fairest flower is she.

'And when she goes into the house,
    Sit ye upon the whin;
And sit you there and sing our loves
    As she goes out and in.'

Lord William has written a love-letter,
    Put it under his pinion gray;
And he's awa' to Southern land
    As fast as wings can gae.

And first he sang a low, low note,
    And then he sang a clear;
And aye the o'erword of the sang
    Was 'Your Love can no win here.'

    goshawk: a large hawk; *whin*: furze

'Feast on, feast on, my maidens all,
  The wine flows you amang;
While I gang to my shot-window
  And hear yon bonnie bird's sang.'

O first he sang a merry sang,
  And then he sang a grave:
And then he peck'd his feathers gray;
  To her a letter gave.

'Have there a letter from Lord William:
  He says, he sent ye three;
He cannot wait your love longer,
  But for your sake he'll die.'

'I send him the rings from my white fingers,
  The garlands of my hair;
I send him the heart that's in my breast;
  What would my love have mair?
And at Mary's kirk in fair Scotland,
  Ye'll bid him wait for me there.'

She hied her to her father dear
  As fast as go could she:
'An asking, an asking, my father dear,
  An asking grant you me!
That if I die in fair England,
  In Scotland bury me.

'At the first kirk of fair Scotland,
  You cause the bells be rung;
At the second kirk of fair Scotland,
  You cause the mass be sung;

'And when you come to Saint Mary's kirk,
   Ye'll tarry there till night.'
And so her father pledged his word,
   And to his promise plight.

The Lady's gone to her chamber
   As fast as she could fare;
And she has drunk a sleepy draught
   That she had mix'd with care.

And pale, pale, grew her rosy cheek,
   And pale and cold was she: –
She seem'd to be as surely dead
   As any corpse could be.

Then spake her cruel stepminnie,
   'Take ye the burning lead,
And drop a drop on her bosom,
   To try if she is dead.'

They dropp'd the hot lead on her cheek,
   They dropp'd it on her chin,
They dropp'd it on her bosom white;
   But she spake none again.

Then up arose her seven brethren,
   And hew'd to her a bier,
They hew'd it from the solid oak;
   Laid it o'er with silver clear.

The first Scots kirk that they came to
   They gart the bells be rung;
The next Scots kirk that they came to
   They gart the mass be sung.

But when they came to Saint Mary's kirk,
    There stood spearmen in a row;
And up and started Lord William,
    The chieftain among them a'.

He rent the sheet upon her face
    A little above her chin;
With rosy cheek and ruby lip,
    She look'd and laugh'd to him.

'A morsel of your bread, my lord!
    And one glass of your wine!
For I have fasted these long days
    All for your sake and mine!'

                    ANONYMOUS

THE RIVER-MERCHANT'S WIFE: A LETTER

While my hair was still cut straight across my forehead
I played about the front gate, pulling flowers.
You came by on bamboo stilts, playing horse,
You walked about my seat, playing with blue plums.
And we went on living in the village of Chokan:
Two small people, without dislike or suspicion.

At fourteen I married My Lord you.
I never laughed, being bashful.
Lowering my head, I looked at the wall.
Called to, a thousand times, I never looked back.

At fifteen I stopped scowling,
I desired my dust to be mingled with yours
Forever and forever and forever.
Why should I climb the look out?

At sixteen you departed,
You went into far Ku-to-en, by the river of swirling eddies,
And you have been gone five months.
The monkeys make sorrowful noise overhead.

You dragged your feet when you went out.
By the gate now, the moss is grown, the different mosses,
Too deep to clear them away!
The leaves fall early this autumn, in wind.
The paired butterflies are already yellow with August
Over the grass in the West garden;
They hurt me. I grow older.
If you are coming down through the narrows
                            of the river Kiang,
Please let me know beforehand,
And I will come out to meet you
   As far as Cho-fu-Sa.

EZRA POUND (1885–1972)

THE LADY'S DIARY

Lectured by Pa and Ma o'er night,
Monday at ten quite vexed and jealous,
Resolved in future to be right,
And never listen to the fellows;

Stitched half a wristband, read the text,
Received a note from Mrs Racket:
I hate that woman, she sat next
All church-time to sweet Captain Clackit.

Tuesday got scolded, did not care,
The toast was cold, 'twas past eleven;
I dreamed the Captain through the air
On Cupid's wings bore me to heaven:
Pouted and dined, dressed, looked divine,
Made an excuse, got Ma to back it;
Went to the play, what joy was mine!
Talked loud and laughed with Captain Clackit.

Wednesday came down no lark so gay,
'The girl's quite altered,' said my mother;
Cried Dad, 'I recollect the day
When, dearee, thou wert such another':
Danced, drew a landscape, skimmed a play,
In the paper read that widow Flackit
To Gretna Green had run away,
The forward minx, with Captain Clackit.

Thursday fell sick: 'Poor soul she'll die';
Five doctors came with lengthened faces;
Each felt my pulse; 'Ah me,' cried I,
'Are these my promised loves and graces?'
Friday grew worse, cried Ma, in pain,
'Our day was fair, heaven do not black it,
Where's your complaint, love?' – 'In my brain.'
'What shall I give you?' – 'Captain Clackit.'

Early next morn a nostrum came
Worth all their cordials, balms and spices;
A letter, I had been to blame;
The Captain's truth brought on a crisis.
Sunday, for fear of more delays,
Of a few clothes I made a packet,
And Monday morn stepped in a chaise
And ran away with Captain Clackit.

CHARLES DIBDIN (1745–1814)

LOCHINVAR

O young Lochinvar is come out of the west,
Through all the wide Border his steed was the best;
And save his good broadsword he weapons had none,
He rode all unarm'd, and he rode all alone.
So faithful in love, and so dauntless in war,
There never was knight like the young Lochinvar.

He staid not for brake, and he stopp'd not for stone,
He swam the Eske river where ford there was none;
But ere he alighted at Netherby gate,
The bride had consented, the gallant came late:
For a laggard in love, and a dastard in war,
Was to wed the fair Ellen of brave Lochinvar.

So boldly he enter'd the Netherby Hall,
Among bride's-men, and kinsmen, and brothers, and all:
Then spoke the bride's father, his hand on his sword,
(For the poor craven bridegroom said never a word),

'O come ye in peace here, or come ye in war,
Or to dance at our bridal, young Lord Lochinvar?'

'I long woo'd your daughter, my suit you denied; –
Love swells like the Solway, but ebbs like its tide –
And now am I come, with this lost love of mine
To lead but one measure, drink one cup of wine.
There are maidens in Scotland more lovely by far,
That would gladly be bride to the young Lochinvar.'

The bride kiss'd the goblet; the knight took it up,
He quaff'd off the wine, and he threw down the cup.
She look'd down to blush, and she look'd up to sigh,
With a smile on her lips, and a tear in her eye.
He took her soft hand, ere her mother could bar, –
'Now tread we a measure!' said young Lochinvar.

So stately his form, and so lovely her face,
That never a hall such a galliard did grace;
While her mother did fret, and her father did fume,
And the bridegroom stood dangling his bonnet and plume;
And the bride-maidens whisper'd, ''Twere better by far
To have match'd our fair cousin with young Lochinvar.'

One touch to her hand, and one word in her ear,
When they reach'd the hall-door, and the charger stood near;
So light to the croupe the fair lady he swung,
So light to the saddle before her he sprung!
'She is won! we are gone, over bank, bush and scaur;
They'll have fleet steeds that follow,' quoth young Lochinvar.

There was mounting 'mong Graemes of the Netherby clan;
Forsters, Fenwicks, and Musgraves, they rode and they ran:
There was racing and chasing on Cannobie Lee,
But the lost bride of Netherby ne'er did they see.
So daring in love, and so dauntless in war,
Have ye e'er heard of gallant like young Lochinvar?

                      SIR WALTER SCOTT
                      (1771–1832)

THE LITTLE GHOST WHO DIED FOR LOVE

Deborah Churchill, born in 1678, was hanged in 1708 for shielding her lover in a duel. His opponent was killed, her lover fled to Holland, and she was hanged in his stead, according to the law at that time. The chronicle said, 'Though she died at peace with God, this malefactor could never understand the justice of her sentence, to the last moment of her life.'

    'Fear not, O maidens, shivering
    As bunches of the dew-drenched leaves
    In the calm moonlight . . . it is the cold sends quivering
    My voice, a little nightingale that grieves.

    Now Time beats not, and dead Love is forgotten . . .
    The spirit too is dead and dank and rotten,

    And I forget the moment when I ran
    Between my lover and the sworded man –

    Blinded with terror lest I lose his heart.
    The sworded man dropped, and I saw depart

Love and my lover and my life . . . he fled
And I was strung and hung upon the tree.
It is so cold now that my heart is dead
And drops through time . . . night is too dark to see

Him still . . . But it is spring; upon the fruit-boughs of your lips,
Young maids, the dew like India's splendour drips,
Pass by among the strawberry beds, and pluck the berries
Cooled by the silver moon; pluck boughs of cherries

That seem the lovely lucent coral bough
(From streams of starry milk those branches grow)
That Cassiopeia feeds with her faint light,
Like Ethiopia ever jewelled bright.

Those lovely cherries to enclose
Deep in their sweet hearts the silver snows

And the small budding flowers upon the trees
Are filled with sweetness like the bags of bees.

Forget my fate . . . But I, a moonlight ghost,
Creep down the strawberry paths and seek the lost

World, the apothecary at the Fair.
I, Deborah, in my long cloak of brown
Like the small nightingale that dances down
The cherried boughs, creep to the doctor's bare
Booth . . . cold as ivy in the air,

And, where I stand, the brown and ragged light
Holds something still beyond, hid from my sight.

Once, plumaged like the sea, his swanskin head
Had wintry white quills . . . "Hearken to the Dead . . .
I was a nightingale, but now I croak
Like some dark harpy hidden in night's cloak
Upon the walls; among the Dead, am quick.
Oh, give me medicine for the world is sick;
Not medicines, planet-spotted like fritillaries
For country sins and old stupidities,
Nor potions you may give a country maid
When she is lovesick . . . love in earth is laid,
Grown dead and rotten" . . . so I sank me down,
Poor Deborah in my long cloak of brown.
Though cockcrow marches, crying of false dawns
Shall bury my dark voice, yet still it mourns
Among the ruins, – for it is not I
But this old world, is sick and soon must die!'

EDITH SITWELL (1887–1964)

FRANKIE AND JOHNNY

Frankie and Johnny were lovers,
O my Gawd how they did love!
They swore to be true to each other,
As true as the stars above,
He was her man but he done her wrong.

Frankie went down to the hock-shop,
Went for a bucket of beer,
Said: 'O Mr Bartender
Has my loving Johnny been here?
He is my man but he's doing me wrong.'

'I don't want to make you no trouble,
I don't want to tell you no lie,
But I saw Johnny an hour ago
With a girl named Nelly Bly,
He is your man but he's doing you wrong.'

Frankie went down to the hotel,
She didn't go there for fun,
'Cause underneath her kimona
She toted a 44 gun.
He was her man but he done her wrong.

Frankie went down to the hotel,
She rang the front-door bell,
Said: 'Stand back all you chippies
Or I'll blow you all to hell.
I want my man for he's doing me wrong.'

Frankie looked in through the key-hole
And there before her eye
She saw her Johnny on the sofa
A-loving up Nelly Bly.
He was her man, he was doing her wrong.

Frankie threw back her kimona,
Took out a big 44,
Root-a-toot-toot, three times she shot
Right through that hardware door.
He was her man but he was doing her wrong.

Johnny grabbed up his Stetson,
Said: 'Oh my Gawd Frankie don't shoot!'
But Frankie pulled hard on the trigger
And the gun went root-a-toot-toot.
She shot her man who was doing her wrong.

'Roll me over easy,
Roll me over slow,
Roll me over on my right side
Cause my left side hurts me so.
I was her man but I done her wrong.'

'Bring out your rubber-tired buggy,
Bring out your rubber-tired hack;
I'll take my Johnny to the graveyard
But I won't bring him back.
He was my man but he done me wrong.

'Lock me in that dungeon,
Lock me in that cell,
Lock me where the north-east wind
Blows from the corner of Hell.
I shot my man 'cause he done me wrong.'

It was not murder in the first degree,
It was not murder in the third.
A woman simply shot her man
As a hunter drops a bird.
She shot her man 'cause he done her wrong.

Frankie said to the Sheriff,
'What do you think they'll do?'
The Sheriff said to Frankie,
'It's the electric-chair for you.
You shot your man 'cause he done you wrong.'

Frankie sat in the jail-house,
Had no electric fan,
Told her sweet little sister:
'There ain't no good in a man.
I had a man but he done me wrong.'

Once more I saw Frankie,
She was sitting in the Chair
Waiting for to go and meet her God
With the sweat dripping out of her hair.
He was her man but he done her wrong.

This story has no moral,
This story has no end,
This story only goes to show
That there ain't no good in men.
He was her man but he done her wrong.

ANONYMOUS
American folk ballad

THE KING-FISHER'S SONG

King Fisher courted Lady Bird –
Sing Beans, sing Bones, sing Butterflies!
   'Find me my match,' he said,
   With such a noble head –
With such a beard, as white as curd –
   With such expressive eyes!'

'Yet pins have heads,' said Lady Bird –
Sing Prunes, sing Prawns, sing Primrose-Hill!
   'And, where you stick them in,
   They stay, and thus a pin
Is very much to be preferred
   To one that's never still!'

'Oysters have beards,' said Lady Bird –
Sing Flies, sing Frogs, sing Fiddle-strings!
   'I love them, for I know
   They never chatter so:
They would not say one single word –
   Not if you crowned them Kings!'

'Needles have eyes!' said Lady Bird –
Sing Cats, sing Corks, sing Cowslip-tea!
   'And they are sharp – just what
   Your Majesty is *not*.
So get you gone – 'tis too absurd
   To come a-courting *me*!'

LEWIS CARROLL (1832–98)
From *Sylvie and Bruno Concluded*

ANTONIO

Antonio, Antonio,
Was tired of living alonio.
   He thought he would woo
   Miss Lissamy Lu,
Miss Lissamy Lucy Molonio.

Antonio, Antonio,
Rode off on his polo-ponio.
   He found the fair maid
   In a bowery shade,
A-sitting and knitting alonio.

Antonio, Antonio,
Said, 'If you will be my ownio,
   I'll love you true,
   And I'll buy for you,
An icery, creamery conio!'

'Oh, *no*nio, Antonio!
You're far too bleak and bonio!
   And all that I wish,
   You singular fish,
Is that you will quickly begonio.'

Antonio, Antonio,
He uttered a dismal moanio;
   Then ran off and hid
   (Or I'm told that he did)
In the Anticatarctical Zonio.

LAURA RICHARDS (1850–1943)

WHY SO PALE AND WAN?

Why so pale and wan, fond lover!
    Prithee, why so pale?
Will, when looking well can't move her,
    Looking ill prevail?
    Prithee, why so pale?

Why so dull and mute, young sinner?
    Prithee, why so mute?
Will, when speaking well can't win her,
    Saying nothing do't?
    Prithee, why so mute?

Quit, quit, for shame! This will not move;
    This cannot take her.
If of herself she will not love,
    Nothing can make her:
    The devil take her!

                    SIR JOHN SUCKLING
                    (1609–41)

Last things

MATTHEW, MARK, LUKE, AND JOHN

Matthew, Mark, Luke, and John,
Bless the bed that I lie on.
Before I lay me down to sleep
I give my soul to Christ to keep.
Four corners to my bed,
Four angels there aspread,
Two to foot, and two to head,
And four to carry me when I'm dead.

I go by sea, I go by land,
The Lord made me with His right hand.
If any danger come to me,
Sweet Jesus Christ deliver me.
He's the branch and I'm the flower,
Pray God send me a happy hour,
And if I die before I wake,
I pray that Christ my soul may take.

ANONYMOUS

EVENING HYMN

The night is come like to the day,
Depart not Thou, great God, away;
Let not my sins, black as the night,
Eclipse the lustre of Thy light.
Keep still in my horizon, for to me
The sun makes not the day, but Thee.

Thou whose nature cannot sleep,
On my temples sentry keep;
Guard me 'gainst those watchful foes,
Whose eyes are open while mine close.
Let no dreams my head infest,
But such as Jacob's temples blest.
While I do rest, my soul advance,
Make my sleep a holy trance:
That I may, my rest being wrought,
Awake into some holy thought.
And with as active vigour run
My course, as doth the nimble sun.
Sleep is a death, O make me try
By sleeping what it is to die.
And as gently lay my head
On my grave, as now my bed.
Now ere I rest, great God, let me
Awake again at last with Thee.
And thus assured, behold I lie
Securely, or to wake or die.
These are my drowsy days, in vain
I do now wake to sleep again.
O come that hour, when I shall never
Sleep again, but wake for ever!

SIR THOMAS BROWNE
(1605–82)

NIGHT

The sun descending in the west,
   The evening star does shine;
The birds are silent in their nest,
   And I must seek for mine.
     The moon, like a flower,
     In heaven's high bower,
     With silent delight
     Sits and smiles on the night.

Farewell, green fields and happy grove,
   Where flocks have took delight:
Where lambs have nibbled, silent move
   The feet of angels bright;
     Unseen they pour blessing,
     And joy without ceasing
     On each bud and blossom,
     On each sleeping bosom.

They look in every thoughtless nest,
   Where birds are cover'd warm;
They visit caves of every beast,
   To keep them all from harm:
     If they see any weeping
     That should have been sleeping,
     They pour sleep on their head,
     And sit down by their bed.

When wolves and tigers howl for prey,
   They pitying stand and weep,
Seeking to drive their thirst away
   And keep them from the sheep.

But, if they rush dreadful,
The angels most heedful,
Receive each mild spirit,
New worlds to inherit.

And there the lion's ruddy eyes
   Shall flow with tears of gold:
And pitying the tender cries,
   And walking round the fold:
      Saying, 'Wrath by His meekness,
      And, by His health, sickness,
      Are driven away
      From our immortal day.

'And now beside thee, bleating lamb,
   I can lie down and sleep,
Or think on Him who bore thy name,
   Graze after thee, and weep.
      For, wash'd in life's river,
      My bright mane for ever,
      Shall shine like the gold
      As I guard o'er the fold.'

WILLIAM BLAKE (1757–1827)

WOLSEY'S FAREWELL

So farewell to the little good you bear me.
Farewell! a long farewell, to all my greatness!
This is the state of man: to-day he puts forth
The tender leaves of hopes; to-morrow blossoms,
And bears his blushing honours thick upon him;
The third day comes a frost, a killing frost;
And, when he thinks, good easy man, full surely
His greatness is a-ripening, nips his root,
And then he falls, as I do. I have ventur'd,
Like little wanton boys that swim on bladders,
This many summers in a sea of glory,
But far beyond my depth: my high-blown pride
At length broke under me, and now has left me,
Weary and old with service, to the mercy
Of a rude stream, that must for ever hide me.
Vain pomp and glory of this world, I hate ye:
I feel my heart new open'd. O! how wretched
Is that poor man that hangs on princes' favours!
There is, betwixt that smile we would aspire to,
That sweet aspect of princes, and their ruin,
More pangs and fears than wars or women have;
And when he falls, he falls like Lucifer,
Never to hope again.

WILLIAM SHAKESPEARE
(1564–1616)
Henry VIII, III ii

ON HIS BLINDNESS

When I consider how my light is spent,
  Ere half my days, in this dark world and wide,
  And that one talent which is death to hide,
Lodged with me useless, though my soul more bent
To serve therewith my Maker, and present
  My true account, lest He returning chide;
  Doth God exact day-labour, light denied,
I fondly ask; – but Patience to prevent
That murmur, soon replies, God doth not need
  Either man's work, or His own gifts; who best
  Bear His mild yoke, they serve Him best: His state
Is kingly. Thousands at His bidding speed
  And post o'er land and ocean without rest:
    They also serve who only stand and wait.

JOHN MILTON (1608–74)

WHEN I HAVE FEARS THAT I MAY CEASE TO BE

When I have fears that I may cease to be
Before my pen has glean'd my teeming brain,
Before high-pilèd books, in charact'ry,
Hold like rich garners the full-ripen'd grain;
When I behold, upon the night's starr'd face,
Huge cloudy symbols of a high romance,
And feel that I may never live to trace
  Their shadows, with the magic hand of chance;
And when I feel, fair creature of an hour!
That I shall never look upon thee more,

Never have relish in the faery power
Of unreflecting love: – then on the shore
  Of the wide world I stand alone, and think,
Till Love and Fame to nothingness do sink.

JOHN KEATS (1795–1821)

From ADONAIS

XL

He has outsoared the shadow of our night;
Envy and calumny, and hate and pain,
And that unrest which men miscall delight,
Can touch him not and torture not again;
From the contagion of the world's slow stain
He is secure, and now can never mourn
A heart grown cold, a head grown grey in vain;
  Nor, when the spirit's self has ceased to burn,
With sparkless ashes load an unlamented urn.

XLI

He lives, he wakes – 'tis Death is dead, not he;
Mourn not for Adonais. – Thou young Dawn,
Turn all thy dew to splendour, for from thee
The spirit thou lamentest is not gone;
Ye caverns and ye forests, cease to moan!
Cease, ye faint flowers and fountains, and thou Air
Which like a mourning veil thy scarf hadst thrown
  O'er the abandoned Earth, now leave it bare
Even to the joyous stars which smile on its despair!

XLII

He is made one with Nature: there is heard
His voice in all her music, from the moan
Of thunder, to the song of night's sweet bird;
He is a presence to be felt and known
In darkness and in light, from herb and stone,
Spreading itself where'er that Power may move
Which has withdrawn his being to its own;
Which wields the world with never-wearied love,
Sustains it from beneath and kindles it above.

XLIII

He is a portion of that loveliness
Which once he made more lovely: he doth bear
His part, while the one Spirit's plastic stress
Sweeps through the dull dense world, compelling there
All new successions to the forms they wear;
Torturing th'unwilling dross that checks its flight
To its own likeness, as each mass may bear;
And bursting in its beauty and its might
From trees and beasts and men into the Heaven's light.

XLIV

The splendours of the firmament of time
May be eclipsed, but are extinguished not:
Like stars to their appointed height they climb,
And death is a slow mist which cannot blot
The brightness it may veil. When lofty thought
Lifts a young heart above its mortal lair,
And love and life contend in it, for what
Shall be its earthly doom, the dead live there
And move like winds of light on dark and stormy air.

PERCY BYSSHE SHELLEY
(1792–1822)

PROUD MAISIE

Proud Maisie is in the wood,
    Walking so early;
Sweet Robin sits on the bush,
    Singing so rarely.

'Tell me, thou bonny bird,
    When shall I marry me?'
'When six braw gentlemen
    Kirkward shall carry ye.'

'Who makes the bridal bed,
    Birdie, say truly?'
'The grey-headed sexton
    That delves the grave duly.

'The glow-worm o'er grave and stone
    Shall light thee steady.
The owl from the steeple sing,
    "Welcome, proud lady."'

SIR WALTER SCOTT
(1771–1832)

OZYMANDIAS

I met a traveller from an antique land
Who said: Two vast and trunkless legs of stone
Stand in the desert . . . Near them, on the sand,
Half sunk, a shattered visage lies, whose frown,
And wrinkled lip, and sneer of cold command,
Tell that its sculptor well those passions read

Which yet survive, stamped on these lifeless things,
The hand that mocked them, and the heart that fed:
And on the pedestal these words appear:
'My name is Ozymandias, king of kings:
Look on my works, ye Mighty, and despair!'
Nothing beside remains. Round the decay
Of that colossal wreck, boundless and bare
The lone and level sands stretch far away.

PERCY BYSSHE SHELLEY
(1792–1822)

ON THE EXTINCTION OF THE VENETIAN REPUBLIC, 1802

Once did she hold the gorgeous East in fee;
And was the safeguard of the West; the worth
Of Venice did not fall below her birth,
Venice, the eldest Child of Liberty.
She was a maiden City, bright and free;
No guile seduced, no force could violate;
And, when she took unto herself a mate,
She must espouse the everlasting Sea.
And what if she had seen those glories fade,
Those titles vanish, and that strength decay;
Yet shall some tribute of regret be paid
When her long life hath reach'd its final day:
Men are we, and must grieve when even the Shade
Of that which once was great is pass'd away.

WILLIAM WORDSWORTH
(1770–1850)

ON WENLOCK EDGE

On Wenlock Edge the wood's in trouble;
   His forest fleece the Wrekin heaves;
The gale, it plies the saplings double,
   And thick on Severn snow the leaves.

'Twould blow like this through holt and hangar
   When Uricon the city stood:
'Tis the old wind in the old anger,
   But then it threshed another wood.

Then, 'twas before my time, the Roman
   At yonder, heaving hill would stare:
The blood that warms an English yeoman,
   The thoughts that hurt him, they were there.

There, like the wind through woods in riot,
   Through him the gale of life blew high;
The tree of man was never quiet:
   Then 'twas the Roman, now 'tis I.

The gale, it plies the saplings double,
   It blows so hard, 'twill soon be gone:
Today the Roman and his trouble
   Are ashes under Uricon.

                                A.E. HOUSMAN (1859–1936)

Uricon: Uriconium – a Roman town on the site of the modern Wroxeter, near Shrewsbury

DIRGE FOR FIDELE

Fear no more the heat o' the sun,
   Nor the furious winter's rages;
Thou thy worldly task hast done,
   Home art gone, and ta'en thy wages;
Golden lads and girls all must
As chimney-sweepers, come to dust.

Fear no more the frown o' the great,
   Thou art past the tyrant's stroke:
Care no more to clothe and eat;
   To thee the reed is as the oak;
The sceptre, learning, physic, must
   All follow this, and come to dust.

Fear no more the lightning-flash,
   Nor the all-dreaded thunder-stone;
Fear not slander, censure rash;
   Thou hast finish'd joy and moan;
All lovers young, all lovers must
   Consign to thee, and come to dust.

No exorciser harm thee!
   Nor no witchcraft charm thee!
Ghost unlaid forbear thee!
   Nothing ill come near thee!
Quiet consummation have;
   And renownèd be thy grave!

WILLIAM SHAKESPEARE
(1564–1616)
Cymbeline, IV ii

REMEMBER

Remember me when I am gone away,
   Gone far away into the silent land;
   When you can no more hold me by the hand,
Nor I half turn to go, yet turning stay.
Remember me when no more day by day
   You tell me of our future that you plann'd:
   Only remember me; you understand
It will be late to counsel then or pray.

Yet if you should forget me for a while
   And afterwards remember, do not grieve:
   For if the darkness and corruption leave
A vestige of the thoughts that once I had,
Better by far you should forget and smile
   Than that you should remember and be sad.

                    CHRISTINA ROSSETTI
                    (1830–94)

REQUIEM

Under the wide and starry sky
   Dig the grave and let me lie:
Glad did I live and gladly die,
   And I laid me down with a will.

This be the verse you grave for me:
Here he lies where he long'd to be;
Home is the sailor, home from sea,
   And the hunter home from the hill.

                    ROBERT LOUIS
                    STEVENSON (1850–94)

I CLIMB THE HILL

I climb the hill: from end to end
  Of all the landscape underneath,
  I find no place that does not breathe
Some gracious memory of my friend;

No gray old grange, or lonely fold,
  Or low morass and whispering reed,
  Or simple stile from mead to mead,
Or sheepwalk up the windy wold;

Nor hoary knoll of ash and haw
  That hears the latest linnet trill,
  Nor quarry trench'd along the hill
And haunted by the wrangling daw;

Nor runlet tinkling from the rock;
  Nor pastoral rivulet that swerves
  To left and right thro' meadowy curves,
That feed the mothers of the flock;
But each has pleased a kindred eye.
  And each reflects a kindlier day;
  And, leaving these, to pass away,
I think once more he seems to die.

ALFRED,
LORD TENNYSON (1809–92)

From *In Memoriam*

HERACLITUS

They told me, Heraclitus, they told me you were dead,
They brought me bitter news to hear and bitter tears to shed.
I wept as I remember'd how often you and I
Had tired the sun with talking and sent him down the sky.

And now that thou art lying, my dear old Carian guest,
A handful of grey ashes, long, long ago at rest,
Still are thy pleasant voices, thy nightingales, awake;
For Death, he taketh all away, but them he cannot take.

WILLIAM (JOHNSON) CORY
(1823–92)

ONE CHRISTMAS-TIME

One Christmas-time,
The day before the holidays began,
Feverish and tired, and restless, I went forth
Into the fields, impatient for the sight
Of those two horses which should bear us home;
My brothers and myself. There was a crag,
An eminence, which from the meeting-point
Of two highways ascending, overlook'd
At least a long half-mile of those two roads,
By which of each the expected steeds might come,
The choice uncertain. Thither I repair'd
Up to the highest summit; 'twas a day
Stormy, and rough, and wild, and on the grass
I sat, half-sheltered by a naked wall;
Upon my right hand was a single sheep,
A whistling hawthorn on my left, and there,

With those companions at my side, I watch'd,
Straining my eyes intensely, as the mist
Gave intermitting prospect of the wood
And plain beneath. Ere I to school return'd
That dreary time, ere I had been ten days
A dweller in my father's house, he died,
And I and my two brothers, orphans then,
Followed his body to the grave. The event
With all the sorrow which it brought appeared
A chastisement, and when I called to mind
That day so lately pass'd, when from the crag
I look'd in such anxiety of hope,
With trite reflections of morality,
Yet in the deepest passion, I bow'd low
To God, who thus corrected my desires;
And afterwards, the wind and sleety rain
And all the business of the elements,
The single sheep and the one blasted tree,
And the bleak music of that old stone wall,
The noise of wood and water, and the mist
Which on the line of each of those two roads
Advanced in such indisputable shapes,
All these were spectacles and sounds to which
I often would repair and thence would drink,
As at a fountain; and I do not doubt
That in this later time, when storm and rain
Beat on my roof at midnight, or by day
When I am in the woods, unknown to me
The workings of my spirit thence are brought.

WILLIAM WORDSWORTH
(1770–1850)
From *The Prelude*, Book XI

A LONDON FETE

All night fell hammers, shock on shock;
With echoes Newgate's granite clang'd:
The scaffold built, at eight o'clock
They brought the man out to be hang'd.
Then came from all the people there
A single cry, that shook the air;
Mothers held up their babes to see,
Who spread their hands, and crow'd for glee;
Here a girl from her vesture tore
A rag to wave with, and join'd the roar;
There a man, with yelling tired,
Stopp'd, and the culprit's crime inquired;
A sot, below the doom'd man dumb,
Bawl'd his health in the world to come;
These blasphemed and fought for places;
Those, half-crush'd, cast frantic faces,
To windows, where, in freedom sweet,
Others enjoy'd the wicked treat.
At last, the show's black crisis pended;
Struggles for better standings ended;
The rabble's lips no longer curst,
But stood agape with horrid thirst;
Thousands of breasts beat horrid hope;
Thousands of eyeballs, lit with hell,
Burnt one way all, to see the rope
Unslacken as the platform fell.
The rope flew tight; and then the roar
Burst forth afresh; still loud, but more
Confused and affrighting than before.
A few harsh tongues for ever led
The common din, the chaos of noises,

But ear could not catch what they said.
As when the realm of the damn'd rejoices
At winning a soul to its will,
That clatter and clangour of hateful voices
Sicken'd and stunn'd the air, until
The dangling corpse hung straight and still.
The show complete, the pleasure past,
The solid masses loosen'd fast:
A thief slunk off, with ample spoil,
To ply elsewhere his daily toil;
A baby strung its doll to a stick;
A mother praised the pretty trick;
Two children caught and hang'd a cat;
Two friends walk'd on, in lively chat;
And two, who had disputed places,
Went forth to fight, with murderous faces.

COVENTRY PATMORE
(1823–96)

BECAUSE I COULD NOT STOP FOR DEATH

Because I could not stop for Death –
He kindly stopped for me –
The carriage held but just ourselves –
And Immortality.

We slowly drove – he knew no haste
And I had put away
My labor and my leisure too,
For his civility.

We passed the school, where children strove
At recess – in the ring –
We passed the fields of gazing grain –
We passed the setting sun –

Or rather – he passed us –
The dews drew quivering and chill –
For only gossamer, my gown –
My tippet – only tulle.

We passed before a house that seemed
A swelling of the ground –
The roof was scarcely visible –
The cornice – in the ground.

Since then – 'tis centuries – and yet
Feels shorter than the day
I first surmised the horses' heads
Were towards Eternity.

EMILY DICKINSON (1830–86)

TO MY DEAR SON, GERVASE BEAUMONT

Can I, who have for others oft compiled
The songs of death, forget my sweetest child,
Which, like a flower crushed, with a blast is dead,
And ere full time hangs down his smiling head,
Expecting with clear hope to live anew,
Among the angels fed with heavenly dew?
We have this sign of joy, that many days,

While on the earth his struggling spirit stays,
The name of Jesus in his mouth contains,
His only food, his sleep, his ease from pains.
O may that sound be rooted in my mind,
Of which in him such strong effect I find.
Dear Lord, receive my son, whose winning love
To me was like a friendship, far above
The course of nature, or his tender age;
Whose looks could all my bitter griefs assuage;
Let his pure soul – ordained seven years to be
In that frail body, which was part of me –
Remain my pledge in heaven, as sent to show
How to this port at every step I go.

SIR JOHN BEAUMONT
(1583–1627)

A QUIET SOUL

Thy soul within such silent pomp did keep,
As if humanity were lull'd asleep;
So gentle was thy pilgrimage beneath,
   Time's unheard feet scarce made less noise,
   Or the soft journey which a planet goes:
Life seem'd all calm as its last breath.
   A still tranquillity so hush'd thy breast,
     As if some Halcyon were its guest,
     And there had built her nest;
It hardly now enjoys a greater rest.

JOHN OLDHAM (1653–83)

JANET WAKING

Beautifully Janet slept
Till it was deeply morning. She woke then
And thought about her dainty-feathered hen,
To see how it had kept.

One kiss she gave her mother
Only a small one gave she to her daddy
Who would have kissed each curl of his shining baby;
No kiss at all for her brother.

'Old Chucky, old Chucky!' she cried,
Running across the world upon the grass
To Chucky's house, and listening. But alas,
Her Chucky had died.

It was a transmogrifying bee
Came droning down on Chucky's old bald head
And sat and put the poison. It scarcely bled,
But how exceedingly

And purply did the knot
Swell with the venom and communicate
Its rigor! Now the poor comb stood up straight
But Chucky did not.

So there was Janet
Kneeling on the wet grass, crying her brown hen
(Translated far beyond the daughters of men)
To rise and walk upon it.

And weeping fast as she had breath
Janet implored us, 'Wake her from her sleep!'
And would not be instructed in how deep
Was the forgetful kingdom of death.

JOHN CROWE RANSOM
(1888–1974)

THE CHILD DYING

Unfriendly friendly universe,
I pack your stars into my purse,
And bid you, bid you so farewell.
That I can leave you, quite go out,
Go out, go out beyond all doubt,
My father says, is the miracle.

You are so great, and I so small:
I am nothing, you are all:
Being nothing, I can take this way.
Oh I need neither rise nor fall,
For when I do not move at all
I shall be out of all your day.

It's said some memory will remain
In the other place, grass in the rain,
Light on the land, sun on the sea,
A flitting grace, a phantom face,
But the world is out. There is no place
Where it and its ghost can ever be.

Father, father, I dread this air
Blown from the far side of despair,
The cold cold corner. What house, what hold,
What hand is there? I look and see
Nothing-filled eternity,
And the great round world grows weak and old.

Hold my hand, oh hold it fast –
I am changing! – until at last
My hand in yours no more will change,
Though yours change on. You here, I there,
So hand in hand, twin-leafed despair –
I did not know death was so strange.

EDWIN MUIR (1887–1959)

AFTERWARDS

When the Present has latched its postern behind my tremulous stay,
   And the May month flaps its glad green leaves like wings,
Delicate-filmed as new-spun silk, will the neighbours say,
   'He was a man who used to notice such things'?

If it be in the dusk when, like an eyelid's soundless blink,
   The dewfall-hawk comes crossing the shades to alight
Upon the wind-warped upland thorn, a gazer may think,
   'To him this must have been a familiar sight.'

If I pass during some nocturnal blackness, mothy and warm,
　　When the hedgehog travels furtively over the lawn,
One may say, 'He strove that such innocent creatures should come
　　　　　　　　　　　　　　　　　　　　　　　　to no harm,
　　But he could do little for them; and now he is gone.'

If, when hearing that I have been stilled at last, they stand at the door,
　　Watching the full-starred heavens that winter sees,
Will this thought rise on those who will meet my face no more,
　　'He was one who had an eye for such mysteries'?

And will any say when my bell of quittance is heard in the gloom,
　　And a crossing breeze cuts a pause in its outrollings,
Till they rise again, as they were a new bell's boom,
　　'He hears it not now, but used to notice such things'?

　　　　　　　　　　　　　　　THOMAS HARDY (1840–1928)

THE GARDEN SEAT

Its former green is blue and thin,
And its once firm legs sink in and in;
Soon it will break down unaware.
Soon it will break down unaware.

At night when reddest flowers are black
Those who once sat thereon come back;
Quite a row of them sitting there.
Quite a row of them sitting there.

With them the seat does not break down,
Nor winter freeze them, nor floods drown,
For they are as light as upper air,
They are as light as upper air!

>   THOMAS HARDY (1840–1928)

IN A DISUSED GRAVEYARD

The living come with grassy tread
To read the gravestones on the hill;
The graveyard draws the living still,
But never any more the dead.

The verses in it say and say:
'The ones who living come today
To read the stones and go away
Tomorrow dead will come to stay.'

So sure of death the marble's rhyme,
Yet can't help marking all the time
How no one dead will seem to come.
What is it men are shrinking from?

It would be easy to be clever
And tell the stones: Men hate to die
And have stopped dying now forever.
I think they would believe the lie.

>   ROBERT FROST (1874–1963)

PROSPERO'S FAREWELL TO HIS MAGIC

Our revels now are ended. These our actors,
As I foretold you, were all spirits and
Are melted into air, into thin air:
And, like the baseless fabric of this vision,
The cloud-capp'd towers, the gorgeous palaces,
The solemn temples, the great globe itself,
Yea, all which it inherit, shall dissolve
And, like this insubstantial pageant faded,
Leave not a rack behind. We are such stuff
As dreams are made on, and our little life
Is rounded with a sleep.

> WILLIAM SHAKESPEARE
> (1564–1616)
> *The Tempest*, IV i

MACBETH ON LADY MACBETH'S DEATH

To-morrow, and to-morrow, and to-morrow,
Creeps in this petty pace from day to day,
To the last syllable of recorded time;
And all our yesterdays have lighted fools
The way to dusty death. Out, out, brief candle!
Life's but a walking shadow, a poor player,
That struts and frets his hour upon the stage
And then is heard no more; it is a tale
Told by an idiot, full of sound and fury,
Signifying nothing.

> WILLIAM SHAKESPEARE
> (1564–1616)
> *Macbeth*, V v

PEACE

My soul, there is a country
    Far beyond the stars,
Where stands a wingèd sentry
    All skilful in the wars,
There above noise and danger
    Sweet Peace sits crown'd with smiles,
And One born in a manger
    Commands the beauteous files.
He is thy gracious Friend,
    And (O my soul, awake!)
Did in pure love descend
    To die here for thy sake,
If thou canst get but thither,
    There grows the flower of Peace,
The Rose that cannot wither,
    Thy fortress, and thy ease;
Leave then thy foolish ranges;
    For none can thee secure,
But One, who never changes,
    Thy God, thy life, thy cure.

HENRY VAUGHAN (1621–95)

TO A POET A THOUSAND YEARS HENCE

I who am dead a thousand years,
    And wrote this sweet archaic song,
Send you my words for messengers
    The way I shall not pass along.

I care not if you bridge the seas,
   Or ride secure the cruel sky,
Or build consummate palaces
   Of metal or of masonry.

But have you wine and music still,
   And statues and a bright-eyed love,
And foolish thoughts of good and ill,
   And prayers to them who sit above?

How shall we conquer? Like a wind
   That falls at eve our fancies blow,
And old Maeonides the blind
   Said it three thousand years ago.

O friend unseen, unborn, unknown,
   Student of our sweet English tongue,
Read out my words at night, alone!
   I was a poet, I was young.

Since I can never see your face,
   And never shake you by the hand,
I send my soul through time and space,
   To greet you. You will understand.

JAMES ELROY FLECKER
(1884–1915)

Maeonides: the Greek poet, Homer

Acknowledgments

Gwendolyn Brooks for 'The Ballad of Rudolph Reed'. Curtis Brown Ltd for Ogden Nash, 'Daddy's Home, See you To-morrow'; 'It is indeed Spinach'; 'Children's Party' and 'It's Never Fair Weather'; Anthony Thwaite, 'White Snow', 'Hedgehog'. Little Brown and Company for Emily Dickinson, 'Answer July'. Cambridge University Press and Ulli Beier for Ulli Beier, 'Elephant'; 'Kob Antelope'; 'Praise of a Child' and 'Yoruba Lullabies'. Laura Cecil Literary Agency and the James Reeves Estate for James Reeves, 'Spells'. Estate of Padraic Colum, for Padraic Colum, 'An Old Woman of the Woods'. EMI Music Publishing for Dave Goulder, 'Long and Lonely Winter'. Faber and Faber Ltd for Mikhail Yurievich Lermontov, (tr. Frances Cornford and E. Polianowsky Salaman) 'Cossack Lullaby'; Louis MacNeice, 'Autobiography'; Peter Abrahams, 'Me, Colored'. Farrar, Straus & Giroux Inc for Seamus Heaney, 'Blackberry-Picking'; 'Follower'; Philip Larkin, 'First Sight'; Thom Gunn, 'Baby Song'; Louise Bogan, 'The Crossed Apple'; Elizabeth Bishop, 'The Map'. Harcourt Brace and Company for Richard Wilbur, 'Boy at the Window'; 'Francis Jammes: A Prayer to go to Paradise with the Donkeys'; T.S. Eliot, 'Landscapes'; 'The Naming of Cats' and 'Journey of the Magi'. HarperCollins Publishers for Hsi Shu, 'Hot Cakes'; Ch'eng Hsaio, 'Satire on Paying Calls in August' (tr. Arthur Waley) and Brian Patten, 'You'd Better Believe Him'. Harvard University Press for Emily Dickinson, 'Because I could not Stop for Death'; 'The Wind Began to Rock the Grass' and 'I Like to See it Lap the Miles'. Henry Holt and Company, Inc for Robert Frost, 'The Oven Bird'; 'Birches'; 'The Road Not Taken' and 'In a Disused Graveyard'. David Higham Associates for Edith Sitwell, 'The Little Ghost who Died for Love'; 'Polka'; Charles Causley, 'Carol of Birds, Beasts and Men', 'At Candlemas', 'Who?' and 'Miller's End'; Elizabeth Jennings, 'The Secret Brother'. Michael Imison Playwrights Ltd for Noel Coward, 'The Boy Actor'. Alfred A. Knopf, Inc for Langston Hughes, 'Negro'; 'Aunt Sue's Stories' and 'Danse Africaine'; John Crowe Ransom, 'Blue Girls'; 'Janet Waking'; Sylvia Plath, 'Mushrooms'. The Lilliput Press for Robin Flower, 'Pangur Bán'. Liveright Publishing Corporation for Robert Hayden, 'Runagate, Runagate'; 'A Road to Kentucky'.

Mrs Mary Martin for Helen Waddell, 'Down from the Branches'. The Marvell Press for Philip Larkin, 'At Grass'. John Murray for John Betjeman, 'Harvest Hymns'; 'Indoor Games near Newbury' and 'Hunter Trials'. New Directions for Ezra Pound, 'The River-Merchant's Wife: A Letter'. University Press of New England for Donald Justice, 'On the Death of Friends in Childhood'. Oxford University Press for 'White Bird Featherless'; 'The Fox's Raid'; 'I Have Four Sisters'; 'The Cuckoo is a Merry Bird'; 'The Key of the Kingdom' and 'Dick Turpin's Ride on Black Bess'. Oxford University Press, Inc for Edwin Muir 'The Child Dying'. Penguin Books Ltd for 'The Man in the Wilderness'. Penguin USA for Ted Hughes, 'Harvest Moon'. Random House, Inc for W. H. Auden, 'Night Mail'. Random House UK Ltd for William Plomer, 'A Victorian Album'; Frances Cornford, 'Travelling Home'; 'Childhood' and 'Acrostic for Guy Fawkes Night'; Norman MacCaig, 'Praise of a Collie'. Richard Rieu for E.V. Rieu, 'Sir Smashum Uppe'. Charles Scribner's Sons for David McCord, 'The Game'; 'Crows'. Stainer & Bell Ltd for Sydney Carter, 'Lord of the Dance'. The Literary Trustees of Walter de la Mare, and the Society of Authors as their representative for Walter de la Mare, 'Song of the Mad Prince' and 'The Scarecrow' and as the literary representative of the Estate of John Masefield for John Masefield, 'The Rider at the Gate'.

Every effort has been made to trace copyright holders of material in this book. The publishers apologize if any material has been included without permission and would be glad to be told of anyone who has not been consulted.

NOTES
RHYMES AND NONSENSE

page 3   *Gray Goose.* An ancient rhyme, first printed in James Orchard Halliwell: *The Nursery Rhymes of England* (1844).

page 3   *The Boatman.* An American round, sent to Iona Opie by a correspondent who learnt it at a girl scout camp *c.* 1938. Printed in *Tail Feathers from Mother Goose: the Opie Rhyme Book*, ed. Iona Opie (1988).

page 3   *I Had a Little Castle.* From *Songs for the Nursery*, published by Benjamin Tabart, 1805.

page 4   *The Owl.* Walter de la Mare in his anthology *Tom Tiddler's Ground* (1932) refers to the legend of the baker's daughter who was turned into an owl. The story goes that Christ had come and asked for bread, and the girl, crying 'Hoo hoo', had rebuked her mother for giving such a large loaf. Charles Waterton, who included the verse in *Essays on Natural History* (1838) said: 'Our nursery maid used to sing it.'

page 5   *The Man in the Wilderness.* This version, with blackberries instead of the more usual strawberries, comes from the *Puffin Book of Magic Verse*, ed. Charles Causley (1974). James Orchard Halliwell used only the first verse in his 1843 compilation, as have most other collectors.

page 6   *I'll Bark against the Dog-Star.* A bedlamite ballad from *Wit and Drollery*, 1682. Songs such as these were sung by seventeenth-century beggars posing as bedlamites or madmen.

page 6   *The Merry Bells of London.* A version of 'Oranges and Lemons' from *Gammer Gurton's Garland*, 1810.

page 8   *Upon Paul's Steeple.* This rhyme first appears in Edward Rimbault's *Nursery Rhymes* (1846). St Paul's cathedral once had a steeple, which was destroyed by lightning in 1561.

page 8   *Trip upon Trenchers.* A dance song, once popular at weddings. From *Mother Goose's Melody*, *c.* 1765.

page 9   *A Man of Words.* From *Gammer Gurton's Garland* (1810).

page 9 *White Bird Featherless*. An ancient riddle of the snow and the sun which has been known in northern Europe since the ninth century. This version comes from Iona and Peter Opie: *Oxford Dictionary of Nursery Rhymes* (1951).

page 10 *The Key of the Kingdom*. From Iona and Peter Opie: *Oxford Nursery Rhyme Book* (1955).

page 11 *The Frog and Mouse*. An eighteenth-century ballad; this version comes from *Gammer Gurton's Garland* (1810).

page 12 *Three Young Rats*. From *The Land of Nursery Rhyme*, ed. Ernest Rhys (1932).

page 13 *The Fox's Raid*. From Opie: *Oxford Dictionary of Nursery Rhymes*.

page 14 *The Drunkard and the Pig*. From the *Oxford Book of American Light Verse*, ed. William Harmon (1979).

page 15 *Black Sheep*. Orally transmitted by A.O.J. Cockshut.

page 15 *Sisters*. From *The Kingfisher Book of Comic Verse*, ed. Roger McGough (1986).

page 16 *There was a Monkey*. From James Orchard Halliwell: *The Nursery Rhymes of England* (1843).

page 21 *The Owl and the Eel and the Warming-Pan*. From *Tirra Lirra* (1933).

page 24 *The Foolish Boy*. From Cecil Sharp: *English Folk Songs from the Southern Appalachians*, vol. II (1932).

page 25 *I Sometimes Think*. Orally transmitted by A.O.J. Cockshut.

page 29 *The Eddystone Light*. The Eddystone lighthouse is at the W end of the English Channel, SW of Plymouth. 'Seven-up accordin' to Hoyle': a game played according to the rules set down by Edmond Hoyle (1672–1769), an authority on card games.

THE YEAR AND ITS SEASONS

page 33 *It's Never Fair Weather*. From *The Funniest Verse of Ogden Nash*, 1968.

page 34 *A New Year Carol*. Children used to sing this carol from door to door on New Year's Eve. The original meaning of the presumably garbled words has been lost in the mists of time. Walter de la Mare included it in *Tom Tiddler's Ground* and Britten set it to music in *Friday Afternoons*.

page 36   *The Eve of St Agnes*. The opening two verses of a forty-two verse poem.

page 42   *Ceremonies for Candlemass Eve*. Candlemas, 2 February, is the feast of the Purification of the Virgin Mary, the day on which the church candles are blessed.

page 47   *Mirth*. From Christopher Smart: *Hymns for the Amusement of Children* (1771). The subject is especially poignant when one remembers that Smart, who was mentally ill, was in prison for debt when the book was published, and died a few months later.

page 50   *The Oven Bird*. The oven bird is a North American warbler. Its song is described as a ringing 'teacher, teacher, teacher'.

page 58   *The Long and Lonely Winter*. The words of a song composed by Dave Goulder, a drystone dyker in the north of Scotland. From the *Oxford Book of Traditional Verse*, ed. Frederick Woods (1979).

page 62   *New Prince, New Pomp*. Robert Southwell was a Jesuit, arrested in 1592 on his way to say mass, repeatedly tortured and finally put to death in 1595. Most of his poems were written in prison.

JOURNEYS AND PLACES

page 69   *The Shepherd Boy's Carol*. Sixteenth century, from a MS in Balliol College, Oxford. Printed in *A Selection of English Carols*, ed. Richard L. Greene (1962). The spelling has been modernized.

page 73   *Runagate, Runagate*. Part I of a poem by a black American poet describing the attempts of his slave ancestors in the South to escape to the North. Pompey was a name often given to a slave. From *Angle of Ascent* (1975).

page 74   *Stanley Meets Mutesa.* An African poet from Malawi describes an episode that took place during Sir Henry Stanley's expedition to central Africa 1874–7. Mutesa was king of the Ganda tribe in East Africa. From *Darkness and Light*, ed. Peggy Rutherford (1958).

page 82   *The Old Ships.* Flecker imagines the 'talkative, bald-headed seaman' to be Ulysses, on his way home from the Trojan war.

page 86   *Adlestrop.* A village in Gloucestershire. The railway and station have long disappeared, but one of the station signs is preserved in a garden there.

page 88   *American Names.* 'Henry and John were never so': refers to the poets Henry Longfellow and John Greenleaf Whittier. Longfellow in particular, professor of French and Spanish at Harvard, was strongly attracted by European culture. He said of himself that to his youthful imagination 'the Old World was a kind of Holy Land'.

SPELLS, MAGIC AND MYSTERY

page 102   *I Have Four Sisters Beyond the Sea.* For five hundred years, say the Opies, who printed it in the *Oxford Dictionary of Nursery Rhymes*, this ancient song 'has been carried in the wallet of popular memory, and for four of these centuries successfully evaded exposure on the printed page'. A version, without the refrain, appears in a manuscript collection of songs made in the early fifteenth century, and they suggest that it may have been old even then. The refrain that appears here seems to be a garbled memory of pre-Reformation church Latin.

page 119   *Two Corpus Christi Carols.* From *A Selection of English Carols*, ed. Richard L. Greene. The first (set to music by Britten in *Friday Afternoons*) is sixteenth-century (the spelling has been modernized), the second nineteenth-century Scots. Corpus Christi (Lat. the body of Christ) is a feast of the Church in celebration of the Eucharist.

page 121   *Thou Great God.* From *Poems for Black Africa*, ed. Langston Hughes (1963). Xhosa is a language of the people of that name, belonging to the Bantu group of the Niger-Congo family and living in Southern Africa.

STRANGE TALES

page 125   *There was a Lady all Skin and Bone.* From *Gammer Gurton's Garland* (1810).

page 137   *A Road in Kentucky.* From *Angle of Ascent* (1975). See note in JOURNEYS above.

MUSIC AND DANCING

page 143   Milton's masque *Comus* was presented at Ludlow Castle on Michaelmas Day, 1634.

page 150   *The Talking Drums.* Kojo Kyei is a poet from Ghana, born in the early 1930s. From *Poems from Black Africa*.

page 156   *Lord of the Dance.* Words for a song. Sydney Carter, poet and songwriter, is one of the leaders of the Folk Revival. From the *Oxford Book of Traditional Verse*.

BATTLES, SOLDIERS AND PATRIOTS

page 161   *War Song of the Saracens.* The Saracens were nomadic Arab warriors from the Syro-Arabian desert who harassed the borders of the Roman Empire.

page 162   *The Destruction of Sennacherib.* Sennacherib, King of Assyria 705–681 B.C., besieged Jerusalem in the course of his campaigns against the Babylonians and their allies, but was defeated by the pestilence that broke out among his troops. ('And it came to pass that night that the angel of the Lord went out, and smote in the camp of the Assyrians an hundred fourscore and five thousand; and when they arose early in the morning, behold, they were all dead corpses.' (2 *Kings* XIX 35).

page 165   *A Jacobite's Epitaph.* The Jacobites supported the claim of the Catholic James II and his successors to the British throne. After their final defeat in 1745 many of them fled into exile in France or Italy.

page 167   *A St Helena Lullaby.* Napoleon Bonaparte, who threatened the whole of Europe in the early years of the nineteenth century, came to eminence in the French Revolutionary Wars, and took the title of Emperor of France in 1804. His most decisive victory was the battle of Austerlitz in 1805, but in that year the French navy was defeated at Trafalgar. He invaded Russia in 1812 but was defeated by the Russian winter ('the Beresina ice'). After his final defeat at Waterloo in 1815 he was exiled to the island of St Helena where he died in 1821.

page 172   *O Captain! My Captain.* The Captain is Abraham Lincoln, President of the United States, who was assassinated in 1865, after he had led the North to victory in the American Civil War.

BIRDS AND BEASTS

page 181   *The Cuckoo.* This version comes from the *Oxford Dictionary of Nursery Rhymes.*

page 182   *Cuckoo, Cuckoo.* A traditional rhyme set to music by Benjamin Britten in *Friday Afternoons.*

page 185   *The Sandpiper.* Celia Thaxter, an American poet well-known in the last century, grew up on the Isles of Shoals, off the coast of New Hampshire, where her father was lighthouse keeper.

page 200   *Epitaph on a Dormouse.* The author of *Goody Two-Shoes* is not known, though there are theories that it might have been Oliver Goldsmith, who certainly worked for John Newbery, the book's publisher. The epitaph on the dormouse is something he well might have written as a child.

page 201   *Sonnet to a Monkey.* Marjory Fleming, who was described by

R.L. Stevenson as 'one of the noblest works of God', must be the youngest person in the *Dictionary of National Biography*. She left a diary, some letters and verses. From *The Complete Marjory Fleming*, ed. Frank Sidgwick (1934).

page 205 *Elephant, Kob Antelope*. The Yoruba are an African people living principally in SW Nigeria, noted for their music, art and sculpture. From *Yoruba Poetry*, comp. Ulli Beier (1970).

page 206 *Dick Turpin's Ride on Black Bess*. A nineteenth-century ballad collected in Oxfordshire *c*. 1914, commemorating a folk hero. Dick Turpin (1706–39), a notorious robber, after killing his confederate Tom King, rode to York on a stolen horse to escape his pursuers. He was hanged in York in 1739. From the *Oxford Book of Traditional Verse*.

page 209 *The Donkey*. The donkey's 'fierce hour and sweet' was when he carried Christ into Jerusalem on Palm Sunday.

page 210 *A Prayer to go to Paradise with the Donkeys*. Francis Jammes (1868–1938) was a French poet and novelist who wrote about nature and animals.

CHILDHOOD AND YOUTH

page 219 *It is indeed Spinach*. From *I'm a Stranger Here Myself* (1938).
page 220 *Children's Party*. From *The Bad Parent's Book of Verse* (1936).
page 230 *Cossack Lullaby*. The Cossacks were warrior peasants from the S steppelands of Russia and the Ukraine, who served as cavalry under the Tsars. From *Poems from the Russian*, chosen and translated by Frances Cornford and Esther Polianowsky Salaman (1942).

page 232 *To his Son, Vincent Corbet*. Corbet was a merry and convivial man, Bishop of Oxford and then of Norwich. He wrote this poem for his son's third birthday, 10 November 1630. Vincent alas grew to be a scapegrace schoolboy who, John Aubrey said in *Brief Lives*, 'goes begging up and down to gentlemen'.

page 233 *Wishes for his Daughter*. Hugh Peters, who had been a minister in Salem, Massachusetts, returned to England in 1641, and was executed in 1660 for abetting the execution of Charles I. This poem appears in his *A Dying Father's Last Legacy to an Onely Child* (1660); I have never seen it reprinted.

page 234   *Autobiography.* Louis MacNeice was the son of a Belfast clergyman (who later became Bishop of Down)—hence 'wore his collar the wrong way round'.

page 235   *Palm Leaves of Childhood.* Adali-Mortti spent his childhood in Ghana. From *Poems from Black Africa*, see above.

page 236   *Me, Colored.* Taken from Peter Abrahams' autobiography *Tell Freedom* (1954). Coloured, or Cape Coloured, was a term used by the South African government to describe a people of mixed descent, mainly living in W Cape province.

page 242   *The Birched Schoolboy.* This poem appears in a manuscript in the possession of Balliol College, Oxford, and dates from the late sixteenth century. In those days boys went to the university at the age of fifteen or sixteen. From *Early English Text Society*, vol. 32 (1867). The spelling is modernized.

page 247   *The Boy Actor.* Noel Coward, actor and playwright, started his professional career in 1911 as Prince Mussel in *The Goldfish*, one of 'a Star Cast of Wonder Children'. He had very little formal education, and was expelled from one school for biting the headmistress in the arm. From *Not Yet the Dodo* (1967).

page 250   *Daddy's Home.* From *You Can't Get There from Here* (1957).

SOME PEOPLE

page 258   *The Bonnie Earl of Moray.* James Stewart, 2nd Earl of Moray, was murdered by Huntly, hereditary enemy of his house, in 1592, probably on the orders of James VI of Scotland, who was jealous of his favour with the queen.

page 259   *The Looking-Glass.* Elizabeth I (1533–1603) was the younger daughter of Henry VIII. In 1587 she was persuaded to execute her cousin Mary Queen of Scots who was a threat to the

English throne. Robert Dudley, Earl of Leicester, who died the following year, had once been her favourite.

page 268 *The Ballad of Rudolph Reed.* Gwendolyn Brooks is a black poet, brought up in the slums of Chicago.

page 272 *Edward Lear.* Lear was a lonely and diffident man, tormented by terrible depression, and convinced that his ugliness repelled those that met him. He struggled to earn a living as a watercolour painter. Auden imagines him taking refuge in the nonsense of his poems.

page 274 *Peter Goole.* From *New Cautionary Tales* (1930).

page 276 *Sir Smasham Uppe.* From *The Flattered Flying Fish* (1962).

page 278 *Wishes of an Elderly Man.* Sir Walter Raleigh was the first professor of English Literature at Oxford. He wrote this after a garden party—perhaps the one given by the Oxford Vice-Chancellor each June, which is especially tedious. From *Laughter from a Cloud* (1923).

page 279 *Lines to the Head of his College.* The story goes that Thomas Brown was a thoroughly unsatisfactory Oxford undergraduate, and Dr Fell, the Dean of Christ Church, threatened to expel him unless he could translate extempore the epigram by the Latin poet Martial which begins 'Non amo te, Sabidi, nec possum dicere quare'. Whereupon Brown responded with this version.

LOVE AND LOVERS' TALES

page 287 *The Cambric Shirt.* From *Gammer Gurton's Garland* (1810).

page 307 *Frankie and Johnny.* This ballad, known in the mid-nineteenth century, was first printed in 1912. It is thought that it describes the actual murder of a St Louis black man by his mistress.

page 312 *Antonio.* From *Merry-go-round* (1935).

LAST THINGS

page 323   *Adonais.* Written in 1821, 'Adonais' commemorates the death of John Keats, 1795–1821.

page 326   *On the Extinction of the Venetian Republic.* Napoleon put an end to the republic of Venice, and its territories were ceded to Austria. For centuries it had been one of the greatest commercial powers in the world.

page 331   *Heraclitus.* A free translation of an epigram by the Greek poet Callimachus. William Johnson, who later took the name of Cory, was an Eton schoolmaster.

INDEX OF AUTHORS AND TITLES

PETER ABRAHAMS 1919–
Me, Colored 236

GEORMBEEYI ADALI-MORTTI
Palm Leaves of Childhood 235

ANONYMOUS: ballads
The Bonnie Earl of Moray 258
Dick Turpin's Ride on Black Bess 206
The Foolish Boy 24
The Fox's Raid 13
Frankie and Johnny 307
The Frog and the Mouse 11
The Gay Goshawk 297
Hynd Horn 294
Strange Company 128
The Wife of Usher's Well 126

ANONYMOUS: nursery rhymes
The Cambric Shirt 287
Gray Goose 3
I Had a Little Castle 3
I Have Four Sisters Beyond the Sea 102
The Key of the Kingdom 10
The Man in the Wilderness 5
A Man of Words 9
Matthew, Mark, Luke, and John 317
The Merry Bells of London 6
There was a Lady all Skin and Bone 125
There was a Monkey 16
Three Young Rats 12
Trip upon Trenchers 8
Upon Paul's Steeple 8

White Bird Featherless 9

ANONYMOUS: songs
The Bellman's Song 4
The Boatman 3
Clementine 28
Two Corpus Christi Carols 119
A Daughter's Song 249
The Eddystone Light 29
I Know Where I'm Going 285
A New Year Carol 34
The Owl 4
The Shepherd Boy's Carol 69
Sweet Suffolk Owl 183
The Water is Wide 286
Western Wind 283

ANONYMOUS: miscellaneous
The Birched Schoolboy 242
Black Sheep 15
Bridal Morning 283
The Common Cormorant 26
Cuckoo, Cuckoo 182
The Cuckoo is a Merry Bird 181
The Drunkard and the Pig 14
Epitaph on a Dormouse 200
I Sometimes Think 25
I'll Bark against the Dog-Star 6
Sisters 15

ANONYMOUS: from the Gaelic, trans. Robin Flower
Pangur Bán 195

ANONYMOUS: from the Latin, trans. Helen Waddell
Down from the Branches 284

358

ANONYMOUS: from the Xhosa, trans. A.C. Jordan
Thou Great God 121

ANONYMOUS: from the Yoruba, trans. Ulli Beier
Elephant 205
Kob Antelope 205
Lullabies 228–9
Praise of a Child 224

W.H. AUDEN 1907–73
Edward Lear 272
Night Mail 84

SIR JOHN BEAUMONT 1583–1627
To my dear Son, Gervase Beaumont 335

HILAIRE BELLOC 1870–1953
The Frog 201
Peter Goole, who Ruined his Father and Mother by his
Extravagance 274
The Python 202
Tarantella 153

STEPHEN VINCENT BENET 1898–1943
American Names 88

SIR JOHN BETJEMAN 1906–84
Harvest Hymn 57
Hunter Trials 223
Indoor Games near Newbury 221

ELIZABETH BISHOP 1911–79
The Map 91

WILLIAM BLAKE 1757–1827
The Echoing Green 225
Laughing Song 227

Night 319
The Schoolboy 243
The Tyger 204

LOUISE BOGAN 1897–1970
The Crossed Apple 291

ROBERT BRIDGES 1844–1930
London Snow 37

GWENDOLYN BROOKS 1917–
The Ballad of Rudolph Reed 268

THOMAS BROWN 1663–1704
Lines to the Head of his College 279

SIR THOMAS BROWNE 1605–82
Evening Hymn 317

ROBERT BROWNING 1812–89
The Patriot 166

GEORGE GORDON, LORD BYRON 1788–1824
The Destruction of Sennacherib 162
The Eve of Waterloo 169
Napoleon's Farewell 171

HENRY CAREY d. 1743
Sally in Our Alley 288

LEWIS CARROLL 1832–98
The King-Fisher's Song 311
The Mock Turtle's Song 149
The Three Badgers 18

SYDNEY CARTER 1915–
Lord of the Dance 156

CHARLES CAUSLEY 1917–
At Candlemas 43
Carol of Birds, Beasts and Men 213
Miller's End 134
Who? 251

CH'ENG HSAIO *c.* 220–64
Satire on Paying Calls in August 51

G.K. CHESTERTON 1874–1936
The Donkey 209
The Rolling English Road 81

COLLEY CIBBER 1671–1757
The Blind Boy 261

JOHN CLARE 1793–1864
Autumn 59
Autumn Birds 184
Hares at Play 189
Spring 46
The Vixen 188

SAMUEL TAYLOR COLERIDGE 1772–1834
Epigram on a Singer 277
Kubla Khan 108

PADRAIC COLUM 1881–1972
An Old Woman of the Roads 266

RICHARD CORBET 1582–1635
To his Son, Vincent Corbet 232

FRANCES CORNFORD 1886–1960
Acrostic for Guy Fawkes Night 61
Childhood 238
Post-Bore Triolet 278

Travelling Home 87

WILLIAM (JOHNSON) CORY 1823–92
Heraclitus 331

SIR NOEL COWARD 1899–1973
The Boy Actor 247

WILLIAM COWPER 1731–1800
Epitaph on a Hare 198

THOMAS DEKKER 1570?–1641?
Lullaby 229

WALTER DE LA MARE 1873–1956
The Scarecrow 41
Song of the Mad Prince 110

CHARLES DIBDIN 1745–1814
The Lady's Diary 301

EMILY DICKINSON 1830–86
Answer July 49
Because I Could Not Stop For Death 334
I Like to See it Lap the Miles 83
The Spider 187
The Wind Began to Rock the Grass 53

JOHN DONNE 1572?–1631
Song 107

JOHN DRYDEN 1631–1700
From Song for St Cecilia's Day 145

T.S. ELIOT 1888–1965
Journey of the Magi 71
Landscapes 95
The Naming of Cats 197

JAMES ELROY FLECKER 1884–1915
The Old Ships 82
To a Poet a Thousand Years Hence 343
War Song of the Saracens 161

MARJORY FLEMING 1803–11
Sonnet to a Monkey 201

ROBERT FROST 1874–1963
Birches 245
In a Disused Graveyard 341
The Oven Bird 50
The Road Not Taken 77

OLIVER GOLDSMITH 1730?–1774
An Elegy on the Death of a Mad Dog 190
The Village Schoolmaster 263

DAVE GOULDER 1939–
The Long and Lonely Winter 58

ROBERT GRAVES 1895–1985
Star-Talk 40

THOMAS GRAY 1716–71
Ode on the Death of a Favourite Cat 193

THOM GUNN 1929–
Baby Song 227

IVOR GURNEY 1890–1937
When March Blows 44

THOMAS HARDY 1840–1928
Afterwards 339
Birds at Winter Nightfall 39
The Garden Seat 340
The Oxen 213

Weathers 45
Winter in Durnover Field 39

ROBERT HAYDEN 1913–80
A Road in Kentucky 137
From Runagate, Runagate 73

SEAMUS HEANEY 1939–
Blackberry-Picking 52
Follower 279

GEORGE HERBERT 1593–1633
Christmas 64

ROBERT HERRICK 1591–1674
Ceremonies for Candlemass Eve 42
Ceremonies for Christmas 63
Epitaph upon a Child that Died 252
To his Saviour, a Child 225

JAMES HOGG 1770–1835
Kilmeny's Return from the Land of the Spirits 130

GERARD MANLEY HOPKINS 1844–89
Binsey Poplars 94

A.E. HOUSMAN 1859–1936
On Wenlock Edge 327

LANGSTON HUGHES 1902–67
Aunt Sue's Stories 267
Danse Africaine 152
Negro 265

TED HUGHES 1930–
The Harvest Moon 55

ELIZABETH JENNINGS 1926–
The Secret Brother 135

BEN JONSON 1572/3–1637
A Catch 5
Epitaph on Salathiel Pavy 260
The Witches' Charms 112

DONALD JUSTICE 1925–
On the Death of Friends in Childhood 253

JOHN KEATS 1795–1821
To Autumn 54
From The Eve of St Agnes 36
When I Have Fears That I May Cease To Be 322

RUDYARD KIPLING 1865–1936
The Coward 175
The Looking-Glass 259
A St Helena Lullaby 167
Road-Song of the *Bandar-Log* 203
Tommy 173
The Way Through the Woods 80

KOJO GYINAYE KYEI
The Talking Drums 150

WALTER SAVAGE LANDOR 1775–1864
The Georges 279

PHILIP LARKIN 1922–85
At Grass 207
First Sight 209

EDWARD LEAR 1812–88
Calico Pie 22
The Table and the Chair 20
Self-Portrait of Edward Lear 270

MIKHAIL YURIEVICH LERMONTOV 1814–41
Cossack Lullaby 230

365

VACHEL LINDSAY 1879–1931
Two Old Crows 27

NORMAN MacCAIG 1910–
Praise of a Collie 192

THOMAS BABINGTON, LORD MACAULAY 1800–1859
A Jacobite's Epitaph 165

DAVID McCORD 1897–
Crows 186
The Game 241

LOUIS MacNEICE 1907–63
Autobiography 234

JOHN MASEFIELD 1878–1967
The Rider at the Gate 131

JOHN MILTON 1608–74
From Comus 143
On his Blindness 322

EDWIN MUIR 1887–1959
The Child Dying 338

OGDEN NASH 1902–71
Children's Party 220
Daddy's Home, See You To-morrow 250
It is indeed Spinach 219
It's Never Fair Weather 33

JOHN OLDHAM 1653–83
A Quiet Soul 336

JOHN O'KEEFFE 1747–1833
The Little Plough-Boy 262

WILFRED OWEN 1893–1918
Anthem for Doomed Youth 175
Disabled 176

COVENTRY PATMORE 1823–96
A London Fête 333

BRIAN PATTEN 1946–
You'd Better Believe Him 136

HUGH PETERS 1598–1660
Wishes for his Daughter 233

SYLVIA PLATH 1932–63
Mushrooms 56

WILLIAM PLOMER 1903–73
A Victorian Album 273

ALEXANDER POPE 1688–1744
Epigram on the Collar of a Dog 192

EZRA POUND 1885–1972
The River-Merchant's Wife: A Letter 300

SIR WALTER A. RALEIGH 1861–1922
Wishes of an Elderly Man 278

JOHN CROWE RANSOM 1888–1974
Blue Girls 251
Janet Waking 337

JAMES REEVES 1909–78
Spells 101

LAURA RICHARDS 1850–1943
Antonio 312
The Owl and the Eel and the Warming-Pan 21

E.V. RIEU 1887–1972
Sir Smasham Uppe 276

JAMES WHITCOMB RILEY 1849–1916
Craqueodoom 23
Little Orphant Annie 138

JOHN WILMOT, EARL OF ROCHESTER 1647–80
Impromptu on Charles II 278

CHRISTINA ROSSETTI 1830–94
From Goblin Market 114
Remember 329

JAMES D. RUBADIRI
Stanley Meets Mutesa 74

SIR WALTER SCOTT 1771–1832
Lucy Ashton's Song 108
Pibroch of Donuil Dhu 163
Lochinvar 303
Proud Maisie 325

WILLIAM SHAKESPEARE 1564–1616
Ariel's Songs 103–4
Dirge for Fidele 328
Fairy Songs 104–5
How Sweet the Moonlight Sleeps 143
Macbeth on Lady Macbeth's Death 342
Prospero's Farewell to his Magic 342
Puck's Epilogue 106
The Seven Ages of Man 257
Spring 44
To Me, Fair Friend, You Never Can Be Old 293
Winter 35
Witches' Song 111
Wolsey's Farewell 321

PERCY BYSSHE SHELLEY 1792–1822
From Adonais 323
Hymn of Pan 146
Ozymandias 325

SHU HSI c. 265–306
Hot Cake 35

SIR PHILIP SIDNEY 1554–86
My True Love Hath My Heart 293

DAME EDITH SITWELL 1887–1964
The Little Ghost who Died for Love 305
Polka 154

CHRISTOPHER SMART 1722–71
Mirth 47

ROBERT SOUTHWELL ?1561–95
New Prince, New Pomp 62

ROBERT LOUIS STEVENSON 1850–94
In the Highlands 90
Requiem 329
Romance 290
Windy Nights 114

SIR JOHN SUCKLING 1609–41
Why so Pale and Wan? 313

ALFRED, LORD TENNYSON 1809–92
The Eagle 187
I Climb the Hill 330
From The Lady of Shalott 79
The Owl 183
The Splendour Falls on Castle Walls 148
To-night the Winds Begin to Rise 60

WILLIAM MAKEPEACE THACKERAY 1811–63
A Tragic Story 17

CELIA THAXTER 1835–94
The Sandpiper 185

EDWARD THOMAS 1878–1917
Adlestrop 86
The Green Roads 78
If I Should Ever by Chance 92
What Shall I Give? 93

ANTHONY THWAITE 1930–
Hedgehog 189
White Snow 240

HENRY VAUGHAN 1621–95
Peace 343

WALT WHITMAN 1819–92
O Captain! My Captain! 172
The Ox-Tamer 211

RICHARD WILBUR 1921–
Boy at the Window 239
Francis Jammes: A Prayer to go to Paradise with the Donkeys 210

WILLIAM WORDSWORTH 1770–1850
Composed Upon Westminster Bridge 95
On the Extinction of the Venetian Republic, 1802 326
One Christmas-Time, *from* The Prelude 331
The Solitary Reaper 264
A Summer's Day, *from* The Prelude 48

W.B. YEATS 1865–1939
The Cat and the Moon 196
The Fiddler of Dooney 149
The Stolen Child 117

INDEX OF FIRST LINES

A child is like a rare bud 224
A cold coming we had of it 71
A creature to pet and spoil 205
A flaxen-headed cow-boy, as simple as may be 262
A man of words and not of deeds 9
A Python I should not advise 202
A wife was sitting at her reel ae nicht 128
A windy night was blowing on Rome 131
Across the lonely beach we flit 185
All after pleasures as I rid one day 64
All the world's a stage 257
All night fell hammers, shock on shock 333
All winter through I bow my head 41
Among the taller wood with ivy hung 188
And when that ballad lady went 137
Answer July 49
Antonio, Antonio 312
Are you awake, Gemelli 40
Around the house the flakes fly faster 39
Aunt Liza 236
Aunt Sue has a head full of stories 267
Be kind and tender to the Frog 201
Be quiet child, and do not cry 228
Beautifully Janet slept 337
Because I could not stop for Death 334
Before the Roman came to Rye or out to Severn strode 81
Behold, a silly tender babe 62
Behold her, single in the field 264
Beside yon straggling fence that skirts the way 263
Buzz! quoth the Blue-Fly 5
Calico Pie 22
Call John the boatman 3

371

Can I not sing but hoy	69
Can I, who have for others oft compiled	335
Can you make me a cambric shirt	287
Children's voices in the orchard	95
Christmas Eve, and twelve of the clock	213
Christus natus est! the cock	213
Come, bring with a noise	63
Come unto these yellow sands	103
Cuckoo, Cuckoo	182
Dame, dame! the watch is set	112
'Dick Turpin, bold Dick, hie away' was the cry	206
Do you remember an Inn	153
Down from the branches fall the leaves	284
Down with the rosemary and bays	42
Earth has not anything to show more fair	95
Elephant who brings death	205
Escaped like a swallow	278
Farewell to the Land where the gloom of my glory	171
Fear no more the heat o' the sun	328
Fear not, O maidens, shivering	305
Frankie and Johnny were lovers	307
From the forests and highlands	146
From the private ease of Mother's womb	227
Full fathom five thy father lies	104
Gay go up and gay go down	6
George the First was always reckoned	279
Give me crowding children. A front lawn damp	61
Go and catch a falling star	107
Go, pretty child, and bear this flower	225
God bless our good and gracious King	278
Golden slumbers kiss your eyes	229
Good afternoon, Sir Smashum Uppe!	276
Good people all, of every sort	190

Gray goose and gander	3
He clasps the crag with crooked hands	187
He discovered an old rocking-horse in Woolworth's	136
He has outsoared the shadow of our night	323
He sat in a wheeled chair, waiting for dark	176
Here lies, whom hound did ne'er pursue	198
Here she lies, a pretty bud	252
Here we bring you new water from the well so clear	34
Here we go in a flung festoon	203
Hey, hey, by this day	242
'Hide' was the word, for most of us were hiders	241
How far is St Helena from a little child at play?	167
How pleasant to know Mr Lear!	270
How sweet the moonlight sleeps upon this bank!	143
Hynd Horn fair, and Hynd Horn free	294
I always found my daughters' beaux	250
I am a Negro	265
I am his Highness' dog at Kew	192
I and Pangur Bán, my cat	195
I can remember, I can remember	247
I climb the hill: from end to end	330
I could not look on Death, which being known	175
I dance and dance without any feet	101
I danced in the morning	156
I do not like the winter wind	33
I do not love you, Dr Fell	279
I had a little castle upon the seaside	3
I have fallen in love with American names	88
I have four sisters beyond the sea	102
I have seen old ships sail like swans asleep	82
I hear the beat	150
I know where I'm going	285
I like to see it lap the Miles	83

I like to walk	186
I love the fitful gust that shakes	59
I love to rise in a summer morn	243
I met a traveller from an antique land	325
I sometimes think I'd rather crow	25
I used to think that grown-up people chose	238
I went into a public-'ouse to get a pint o' beer	173
I who am dead a thousand years	343
I will make you brooches and toys for your delight	290
I wish I loved the Human Race	278
I wish your lamp and vessel	233
I'll bark against the Dog-star	6
I've come to give you fruit from out my orchard	291
If Candlemas is fine and clear	43
If I should ever by chance grow rich	92
If only I hadn't had sisters	15
If you are merry sing away	47
In a cavern in a canyon, excavating for a mine	28
In a far-away northern country in the placid pastoral region	211
In among the silver birches winding ways of tarmac wander	221
In my childhood trees were green	234
In Paper Case	200
In the highlands, in the country places	90
In Xanadu did Kubla Khan	108
It was roses, roses all the way	166
It's awf'lly bad luck on Diana	223
Its former green is blue and thin	340
It was early last December	14
Jack lived in the green-house	135
King Fisher courted Lady Bird	311
Lambs that learn to walk in snow	209
Land lies in water; it is shadowed green	91
Late August, given heavy rain and sun	52

Lectured by Pa and Ma o'er night	301
Left by his friends to breakfast alone on the white	272
Little Orphant Annie's come to our house to stay	138
Look not thou on beauty's charming	108
Lully, lulley, lully, lulley	119
Maids to bed and cover coal	4
Matriarch, admiral, pert-faced boy	273
Matthew, Mark, Luke, and John	317
May I join you in the doghouse, Rover?	220
Me father was the keeper of the Eddystone Light	29
Morning and evening	114
My aspens dear, whose airy cages quelled	94
My father fain would have me take	249
My father worked with a horse-plough	279
My soul, there is a country	343
My true Love hath my heart, and I have his	293
Now fall asleep, my lovely babe	230
Now the hungry lion roars	106
O Captain! my Captain! our fearful trip is done	172
O lovely O most charming pug	201
O say, what is that thing called light	261
O, to have a little house!	266
O well is me, my gay goshawk	297
O young Lochinvar is come out of the west	303
Of all the girls that are so smart	288
Oh, dear beyond our dearest dreams	19
Oh, many a time have I, a five year's child	48
On either side the river lie	79
On Wenlock Edge the wood's in trouble	327
Once did she hold the gorgeous East in fee	326
Once I was a monarch's daughter	4
One Christmas-time	331
Our revels now are ended. These our actors	342

Over hill, over dale	104
Overnight, very	56
Pale sunbeams gleam	46
People by whom I am riled	219
Pibroch of Donuil Dhu	163
Proud Maisie is in the wood	325
Remember me when I am gone away	329
Rudolph Reed was oaken	268
Runs falls rises stumbles on from darkness into darkness	73
Said the Table to the Chair	20
Season of mists and mellow fruitfulness!	54
Seeing the snowman standing all alone	239
She was a small dog, neat and fluid	192
So farewell to the little good you bear me	321
St Agnes' Eve – Ah, bitter chill it was!	36
Such a time of it they had	74
Summer comes October, the green becomes the brown	58
Swans sing before they die – 'twere no bad thing	277
Sweet Suffolk owl, so trimly dight	183
The Assyrian came down like the wolf on the fold	162
The birds are gone to bed, the cows are still	189
The cat went here and there	196
The common cormorant or shag	26
The Crankadox leaned o'er the edge of the moon	23
The cuckoo is a merry bird	181
The eye can hardly pick them out	207
The flame-red moon, the harvest moon	55
The fox jumped up one winter's night	13
The green roads that end in the forest	78
The heron flew east, the heron flew west	120
The living come with grassy tread	341
The low beating of the tom-toms	152
The maidens came	283

The Man in the Wilderness asked of me	5
The Naming of Cats is a difficult matter	197
The night is come like to the day	317
The Owl and the Eel and the Warming-pan	21
The Queen was in her chamber, and she was middling old	259
The spider holds a silver ball	187
The splendour falls on castle walls	148
The Star that bids the Shepherd fold	143
The sun descending in the west	319
The Sun does arise	225
The train. A hot July. On either hand	87
The water is wide, I cannot get through	286
The wild duck startles like a sudden thought	184
The wind began to rock the grass	53
There be three Badgers on a mossy stone	18
There is a singer everyone has heard	50
There liv'd a sage in days of yore	17
There lived a wife at Usher's Well	126
There was a frog liv'd in a well	11
There was a lady all skin and bone	125
There was a monkey climbed a tree	16
There was a sound of revelry by night	169
There was an old man of Khartoum	15
They shut the road through the woods	80
They told me, Heraclitus, they told me you were dead	331
This is the key of the kingdom	10
This is the Night Mail crossing the Border	84
This is the weather the cuckoo likes	45
Thou great God that dwellest in Heaven	121
Three young rats with black felt hats	12
Thrice the brinded cat hath mew'd	111
Throughout the field I find no grain	39
Thy soul within such silent pomp did keep	336

To me, fair friend, you never can be old	293
To my true king I offer'd free from stain	165
To-morrow, and to-morrow, and to-morrow	342
To-night the winds begin to rise	60
Tra la la la – See me dance the polka	154
Trip upon trenchers, and dance upon dishes	8
'Twas on a lofty vase's side	193
Twirling your blue skirts, travelling the sward	251
Twitching the leaves just where the drainpipe clogs	189
Two old crows sat on a fence rail	27
Two roads diverged in a yellow wood	77
Tyger! Tyger! burning bright	204
Under the wide and starry sky	329
Unfriendly friendly universe	338
Upon Paul's steeple stands a tree	8
We are they who come faster than fate	161
We shall not ever meet them bearded in heaven	253
We spray the fields and scatter	57
Weep with me, all you that read	260
Western wind, when will you blow	283
What I shall leave thee, none can tell	232
What passing-bells for these who die as cattle?	175
What passion cannot Music raise and quell?	145
What shall I give my daughter the younger	93
When cats run home and light is come	183
When daisies pied and violets blue	44
When fishes flew and forests walked	209
When I consider how my light is spent	322
When I have fears that I may cease to be	322
When I must come to you, O my God, I pray	210
When I play on my fiddle in Dooney	149
When I see birches bend to left and right	245
When I was a little boy, I lived by myself	24

When I was very small indeed	235
When I was young, throughout the hot season	51
When icicles hang by the wall	35
When many a day had come and fled	130
When March blows, and Monday's linen is shown	44
When men were all asleep the snow came flying	37
When the green woods laugh with the voice of joy	227
When the present has latched its postern behind my tremulous stay	339
When we moved to Miller's End	134
Whenever the moon and stars are set	114
Where dips the rocky highland	117
Where the bee sucks, there suck I	104
While my hair was still cut straight across my forehead	300
White bird featherless	9
'White snow,' my daughters says, and sees	240
'Will you walk a little faster,' said a whiting to a snail	149
Who is that child I see wandering, wandering	251
Who said, 'Peacock Pie'?	110
Why so pale and wan, fond lover!	313
Winter has come; fierce is the cold	35
Ye Hielands and ye Lawlands	258
Yes, I remember Adlestrop	86
You spotted snakes with double tongue	105
Young Peter Goole, a child of nine	274

GILLIAN AVERY (1926–) was born in Reigate, Surrey, where she started her writing career as a journalist on the *Surrey Mirror*. Deciding that the pace of book publishing was more congenial than that of newspapers, she went to Oxford in 1950 to work for the Clarendon Press. In 1952 she married a don, Anthony Cockshut, and when they moved to Manchester she was so homesick for Oxford that she set her first novel, *The Warden's Niece* (1957), in an Oxford college in Victorian times, feeling an affinity between her own pre-war generation and the Victorian child, characterized by a 'meek acceptance of the power of the adult world'. Returning to Oxford in 1964, she continued to write novels, including *A Likely Lad*, set in Manchester, which won the *Guardian* award for children's fiction in 1971 and was successfully dramatized as a children's TV serial.

Gillian Avery is also well known as a historian of children's literature. Her most recent book, *Behold the Child: American Children and their Books, 1621–1922*, is published by The Bodley Head.

THOMAS BEWICK (1753–1828) was born at Eltringham, Northumberland, the eldest of eight children of a tenant farmer. At fourteen he was apprenticed to Ralph Beilby, a metal engraver in Newcastle, and his talent quickly showed itself, particularly in engraving on wood. He practised his skill first on chapbooks and books for children, and through all his subsequent work in book illustration transformed the technique of wood-cutting into a truly creative art. In 1776 he moved to London but did not like the city and soon returned to Newcastle, where he went into partnership with Beilby, their main business being the engraving of bank notes, coffin plates, door plates and such. In his own time Bewick pursued his interest in natural history, making over three hundred wood blocks for his *General History of Quadrupeds*, published in 1790. This was followed by *The History of British Birds*, published in two parts, 'Land Birds' (1797) and 'Water Birds' (1804). His reputation as a wood engraver is only matched by his knowledge of animals and birds and his intense love of the English countryside.

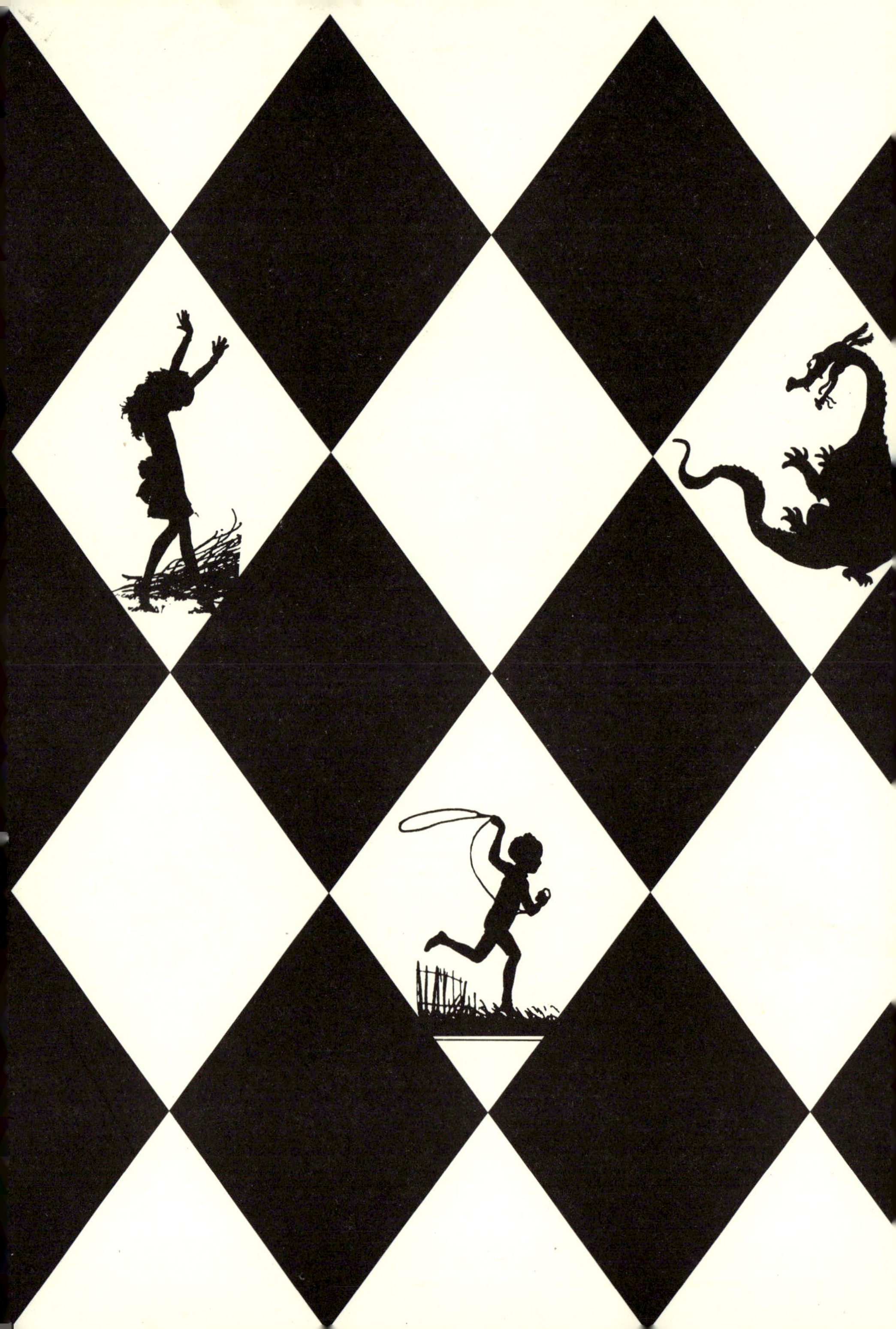